Plus Size Fashions™

Contents

Swinging Pearl JACKET

SKILL LEVEL

INTERMEDIATE

FINISHED SIZES

Instructions given fit size X-large; changes for 2X-large, 3X-large, 4X-large, 5X-large and 6X-large are in [ ].

FINISHED GARMENT MEASUREMENTS

Bust: 48 inches (*X-large*) [52 inches (*2X-large*), 56 inches (*3X-large*), 60 inches (*4X-large*), 64 inches (*5X-large*), 68 inches (*6X-large*]

MATERIALS

- Red Heart Bamboo/Wool medium (worsted) weight bamboo/wool yarn (1¾ oz/87 yds/50g per ball): 19 [21, 23, 25, 27, 28] balls #3650 dill
- Size G/6/4mm crochet hook or size needed to obtain gauge
- Tapestry needle
- Sewing needle
- Sewing thread
- 1¼-inch buttons: 3

GAUGE

9 sc = 2 inches; 6 sc rows = 2 inches

Take time to check gauge.

PATTERN NOTES

Button extensions are crocheted as part of Right and Left Fronts and are included in measurements provided on schematic.

Finished Garment Measurement exclude overlap from button extensions.

Join with slip stitch as indicated unless otherwise stated.

SPECIAL STITCH

Extended single crochet (ext sc): Insert hook in place indicated, yo, pull up lp, yo, pull through 1 lp on hook (first step), yo, pull through all lps on hook.

INSTRUCTIONS
JACKET
BACK

Row 1 (WS): Ch 117 [126, 135, 144, 153, 162], 3 sc in 3rd ch from hook, [sk next 2 chs, 3 sc in next ch] across, turn. (*117 [126, 135, 144, 153, 162] sc*)

Row 2 (RS): Ch 1, sk first sc, *3 sc in next sc**, sk next 2 sc, rep from * across, ending last rep at **, leaving last sc unworked, turn.

Next rows: [Rep row 2] 22 [22, 24, 24, 26, 26] times.

A-LINE SHAPING
Row 1: Ch 1, sk first sc, *[2 sc in next sc, sk next 2 sc]* 3 times, ◊[3 sc in next sc, sk next 2 sc]◊ 15 [17, 18, 19, 21, 22] times, rep between * 3 times, rep between ◊ 15 [16, 18, 20, 21, 23] times, rep between * twice, 2 sc in next sc, leaving last sc unworked, turn. *(108 [117, 126, 135, 144, 153] sc)*

Row 2: Ch 1, sk first sc, *3 sc in next sc**, sk next 2 sc, rep from * across, ending last rep at **, leaving last sc unworked, turn.

Next rows: [Rep row 2] 20 [20, 18, 18, 16, 16] times.

ARMHOLE SHAPING
Row 1: Ch 1, sk first sc, sl st in each of next 8 [8, 11, 11, 14, 14] sc, ch 1, sk next sc, 2 sc in next sc, [sk next 2 sc, 3 sc in next sc] across to last 13 [13, 16, 16, 19, 19] sc, sk next 2 sc, 2 sc in next sc, sk next sc, sl st in next sc, leaving last 8 [8, 11, 11, 14, 14] sc unworked, turn. *(88 [97, 100, 109, 112, 121] sc)*

Row 2: Ch 1, sc in first sc, [sk next 2 sc, 3 sc in next sc] across to last 3 sc, sk next 2 sc, sc in last sc, turn. *(86 [95, 98, 107, 110, 119] sc)*

Row 3: Ch 1, sk first 2 sc, 2 sc in next sc, [sk next 2 sc, 3 sc in next sc] across to last 5 sc, sk next 2 sc, 2 sc in next sc, sk next sc, sl st in last sc, turn. *(82 [91, 94, 103, 106, 115] sc)*

Next rows: [Rep rows 2 and 3 alternately] 1 [2, 2, 4, 4, 5] time(s). *(76 [79, 82, 79, 82, 85] sc)*

UPPER BACK
Row 1: Ch 1, sc in first sc, [sk next 2 sc, 3 sc in next sc] across to last 3 sc, sk next 2 sc, sc in last sc, turn. *(74 [77, 80, 77, 80, 83] sc)*

Row 2: Ch 1, sk first 2 sc, [3 sc in next sc, sk next 2 sc] across, turn. *(72 [75, 78, 75, 78, 81] sc)*

Row 3: Ch 1, sk first sc, *3 sc in next sc**, sk next 2 sc, rep from * across, ending last rep at **, leaving last sc unworked, turn.

Next rows: [Rep row 3] 25 [23, 25, 23, 25, 23] times.

Next row: Ch 1, sk first sc, sl st in each of next 4 sc, ch 1, sk next 2 sc, 2 sc in next sc, [sk next 2 sc, 3 sc in next sc] across to last 10 sc, sk next 2 sc, 2 sc in next sc, sk next 2 sc, sl st in next sc, leaving last 4 sc unworked, turn. *(58 [61, 64, 61, 64, 67] sc)*

LEFT SHOULDER
Row 1: Ch 1, 2 sc in first sc, [sk next 2 sc, 3 sc in next sc] 5 times, sk next 2 sc, 2 sc in next sc, turn. *(19 sc)*

Row 2: Ch 1, 2 sc in first sc, [sk next 2 sc, 3 sc in next sc] 3 times, sk next 2 sc, sc in next sc, leaving last 6 sc unworked, turn. *(12 sc)*

Row 3: Ch 1, sk first 2 sc, 2 sc in next sc, [sk next 2 sc, 3 sc in next sc] twice, sk next 2 sc, 2 sc in last sc. Fasten off. *(10 sc)*

RIGHT SHOULDER
Row 1: With WS facing, sk 19 [22, 25, 22, 25, 28] sc, **join** *(see Pattern Notes)* in next sc, ch 1, 2 sc in next sc, [sk next 2 sc, 3 sc in next sc] 5 times, sk next 2 sc, 2 sc in next sc, turn. *(19 sc)*

Row 2: Ch 1, sk first sc, sl st in each of next 4 sc, ch 1, sk next 2 sc, sc in next sc, [sk next 2 sc, 3 sc in next sc] 3 times, sk next 2 sc, 2 sc in last sc, turn. *(12 sc)*

Row 3: Ch 1, 2 sc in first sc, [sk next 2 sc, 3 sc in next sc] twice, sk next 2 sc, 2 sc in next sc, sk next sc, sl st in next sc. Fasten off. *(10 sc)*

RIGHT FRONT
Row 1 (WS): Ch 63 [69, 72, 78, 81, 87], 3 sc in 3rd ch from hook, [sk next 2 chs, 3 sc in next ch] across, turn. *(63 [69, 72, 78, 81, 87] sc)*

Row 2 (RS): Ch 1, sk first sc, *3 sc in next sc**, sk next 2 sc, rep from * across, ending last rep at **, leaving last sc unworked, turn.

Next rows: [Rep row 2] 22 [22, 24, 24, 26, 26] times.

A-LINE SHAPING

Row 1: Ch 1, sk first sc, *[3 sc in next sc, sk next 2 sc]* 9 [10, 10, 11, 12, 13] times, [2 sc in next sc, sk next 2 sc] 3 times, rep between * 9 [10, 11, 12, 12, 13] times, turn. *(60 [66, 69, 75, 78, 84] sc)*

Row 2: Ch 1, sk first sc, *3 sc in next sc**, sk next 2 sc, rep from * across, ending last rep at **, leaving last sc unworked, turn.

Next rows: [Rep row 2] 14 [14, 10, 12, 8, 8] times.

BUTTONHOLE

Row 1: Ch 1, sk first sc, [3 sc in next sc, sk next 2 sc] 17 [19, 20, 22, 23, 25] times, (2 sc, **ext sc**—*see Special Stitch*) in next sc, ext sc in first step of last ext sc, 2 sc in first step of last ext sc, sk next 5 sc, 3 sc in next sc, sk last sc, turn.

Row 2: Ch 1, sk first sc, *3 sc in next sc**, sk next 2 sc, rep from * across, ending last rep at **, leaving last sc unworked, turn.

Next rows: [Rep row 2] 4 [4, 6, 4, 6, 6] times.

ARMHOLE SHAPING

Row 1: Ch 1, sk first sc, sl st in each of next 8 [8, 11, 11, 14, 14] sc, ch 1, sk next sc, 2 sc in next sc, [sk next 2 sc, 3 sc in next sc] across, sk last sc, turn. *(50 [56, 56, 62, 62, 68] sc)*

Row 2: Ch 1, sk first sc, [3 sc in next sc, sk next 2 sc] across to last 3 sc, sk next 2 sc, sc in last sc, turn. *(49 [55, 55, 61, 61, 67] sc)*

Row 3: Ch 1, sk first 2 sc, 2 sc in next sc, [sk next 2 sc, 3 sc in next sc] across, sk last sc, turn. *(47 [53, 53, 59, 59, 65] sc)*

Rows 4 & 5: Rep rows 2 and 3. *(44 [50, 50, 56, 56, 62] sc at end of last row)*

Row 6: Rep row 2. *(43 [49, 49, 55, 55, 61] sc)*

Row 7: Ch 1, sk first sc, [3 sc in next sc, sk next 2 sc] across, turn. *(42 [48, 48, 54, 54, 60] sc)*

Row 8: Ch 1, sk first sc, *3 sc in next sc**, sk next 2 sc, rep from * across, ending last rep at **, leaving last sc unworked, turn.

Next row: [Rep row 8] 1 [1, 1, 3, 3, 3] time(s).

Next row: Ch 1, sk first sc, (2 sc, ext sc) in next sc, ext sc in first step of last ext sc, 2 sc in first step of last ext sc, sk next 5 sc, [3 sc in next sc, sk next 2 sc] across, sk last sc, turn.

Next rows: [Rep row 8] 14 [14, 16, 16, 18, 18] times.

Next row: Ch 1, sk first sc, [3 sc in next sc, sk next 2 sc] 11 [13, 13, 15, 15, 17] times, (2 sc, ext sc) in next sc, ext sc in first step of last ext sc, 2 sc in first step of last ext sc, sk next 5 sc, 3 sc in next sc, sk last sc, turn.

Next rows: [Rep row 8] twice.

NECKLINE SHAPING

Row 1: Ch 1, sk first sc, sl st in each of next 8 [11, 11, 14, 14, 17] sc, ch 1, sk next sc, 2 sc in next sc, [sk next 2 sc, 3 sc in next sc] across, leaving last sc unworked, turn. *(32 [35, 35, 38, 38, 41] sc)*

Row 2: Ch 1, sk first sc, [3 sc in next sc, sk next 2 sc] across, sc in last sc, turn. *(31 [34, 34, 37, 37, 40] sc)*

Row 3: Ch 1, sk first 2 sc, 2 sc in next sc, [sk next 2 sc, 3 sc in next sc] across, sk last sc, turn. *(29 [32, 32, 35, 35, 38] sc)*

Rows 4 & 5: Rep rows 2 and 3. *(26 [29, 29, 32, 32, 35] sc at end of last row)*

Row 6: Ch 1, sk first sc, [3 sc in next sc, sk next 2 sc] across, 2 sc in last sc, turn.

Row 7: Ch 1, 2 sc in first sc, [sk next 2 sc, 3 sc in next sc] 5 times, sk next 2 sc, sc in next sc, leaving last 7 [10, 10, 13, 13, 16] sc unworked, turn. *(18 sc)*

Row 8: Ch 1, sk first 2 sc, 2 sc in next sc, [sk next 2 sc, 3 sc in next sc] 4 times, sk next 2 sc, 2 sc in last sc, turn. *(16 sc)*

Row 9: Ch 1, 2 sc in first sc, [sk next 2 sc, 3 sc in next sc] 3 times, sk next 2 sc, sc in next sc, leaving last 3 sc unworked, turn. *(12 sc)*

Row 10: Ch 1, sk first 2 sc, 2 sc in next sc, [sk next 2 sc, 3 sc in next sc] twice, sk next 2 sc, 2 sc in last sc. Fasten off. *(10 sc)*

LEFT FRONT

Row 1 (WS): Ch 63 [69, 72, 78, 81, 87], 3 sc in 3rd ch from hook, [sk next 2 chs, 3 sc in next ch] across, turn. *(63 [69, 72, 78, 81, 87] sc)*

Row 2 (RS): Ch 1, sk first sc, *3 sc in next sc**, sk next 2 sc, rep from * across, ending last rep at **, leaving last sc unworked, turn.

Next rows: [Rep row 2] 22 [22, 24, 24, 26, 26] times.

A-LINE SHAPING

Row 1: Ch 1, sk first sc, *[3 sc in next sc, sk next 2 sc]* 9 [10, 11, 12, 12, 13] times, [2 sc in next sc, sk next 2 sc] 3 times, rep between * 9 [10, 10, 11, 12, 13] times, turn. *(60 [66, 69, 75, 78, 84] sc)*

Row 2: Ch 1, sk first sc, *3 sc in next sc**, sk next 2 sc, rep from * across, ending last rep at **, leaving last sc unworked, turn.

Next rows: [Rep row 2] 20 [20, 18, 18, 16, 16] times.

ARMHOLE SHAPING

Row 1: Ch 1, sk first sc, [3 sc in next sc, sk next 2 sc] 16 [18, 18, 20, 20, 22] times, 2 sc in next sc, sk next sc, sl st in next sc, leaving last 8 [8, 11, 11, 14, 14] sc unworked, turn. *(50 [56, 56, 62, 62, 68] sc)*

Row 2: Ch 1, sc in first sc, [sk next 2 sc, 3 sc in next sc] across, sk last sc, turn. *(49 [55, 55, 61, 61, 67] sc)*

Row 3: Ch 1, sk first sc, [3 sc in next sc, sk next 2 sc] across to last 5 sc, sk next 2 sc, 2 sc in next sc, sk next sc, sl st in last sc, turn. *(47 [53, 53, 59, 59, 65] sc)*

Rows 4 & 5: Rep rows 2 and 3. *(44 [50, 50, 56, 56, 62] sc at end of last row)*

Row 6: Rep row 2. *(43 [49, 49, 55, 55, 61] sc)*

Row 7: Ch 1, sk first sc, *3 sc in next sc**, sk next 2 sc, rep from * across, ending last rep at **, sk next sc, sl st in last sc, turn. *(42 [48, 48, 54, 54, 60] sc)*

Row 8: Ch 1, sk first sc, *3 sc in next sc**, sk next 2 sc, rep from * across, ending last rep at **, sk last sc, turn.

Next rows: [Rep row 8] 19 [19, 21, 23, 25, 25] times.

NECKLINE SHAPING

Row 1: Ch 1, sk first sc, [3 sc in next sc, sk next 2 sc] 10 [11, 11, 12, 12, 13] times, 2 sc in next sc, sk next sc, sl st in next sc, leaving last 8 [8, 11, 11, 14, 14] sc unworked, turn. *(32 [35, 35, 38, 38, 41] sc)*

Row 2: Ch 1, sc in first sc, [sk next 2 sc, 3 sc in next sc] across, sk last sc, turn. *(31 [34, 34, 37, 37, 40] sc)*

Row 3: Ch 1, sk first sc, [3 sc in next sc, sk next 2 sc] across to last 3 sc, 2 sc in next sc, sk next sc, sl st in last sc, turn. *(29 [32, 32, 35, 35, 38] sc)*

Rows 4 & 5: Rep rows 2 and 3. *(26 [29, 29 32, 32, 35] sc)*

Row 6: Ch 1, 2 sc first sc, [sk next 2 sc, 3 sc in next sc] across, sk last sc, turn.

Row 7: Ch 1, sk first sc, sl st in each of next 4 [7, 7, 10, 10, 13] sc, ch 1, sk next 2 sc, sc in next sc, [sk next 2 sc, 3 sc in next sc] 5 times, sk next 2 sc, 2 sc in last sc, turn. *(18 sc)*

Row 8: Ch 1, 2 sc in first sc, [sk next 2 sc, 3 sc in next sc] 4 times, sk next 2 sc, 2 sc in next sc, sk last 2 sc, turn. *(16 sc)*

Row 9: Ch 1, sc in first sc, [sk next 2 sc, 3 sc in next sc] 3 times, sk next 2 sc, 2 sc in next sc, sk last sc, turn. *(12 sc)*

Row 10: Ch 1, 2 sc in first sc, [sk next 2 sc, 3 sc in next sc] twice, sk next 2 sc, 2 sc in next sc, sk last 2 sc. Fasten off. *(10 sc)*

SLEEVE
MAKE 2.

Row 1 (WS): Ch 48 [48, 51, 51, 54, 54], 3 sc in 3rd ch from hook, [sk next 2 ch, 3 sc in next ch] across, turn. *(48 [48, 51, 51, 54, 54] sc)*

Row 2 (RS): Ch 1, sk first sc, *3 sc in next sc**, sk next 2 sc, rep from * across, ending last rep at **, sk last sc, turn.

Row 3: Rep row 2.

Row 4: Ch 1, sk first sc, [4 sc in next sc, sk next 2 sc] 3 times, *3 sc in next sc**, sk next 2 sc, rep from * across, ending last rep at **, sk last sc, turn. *(51 [51, 54, 54, 57, 57] sc)*

Row 5: Ch 1, sk first sc, *3 sc in next sc**, sk next 2 sc, rep from * across, ending last rep at **, sk last sc, turn.

Row 6: Rep row 5.

Next rows: [Rep rows 4–6 consecutively] 10 [6, 6, 2, 2, 0] times. *(81 [69, 72, 60, 63, 57] sc at end of last row)*

Next rows: [Rep row 4 twice, rep row 5 twice] 1 [4, 4, 7, 7, 9] time(s). *(87 [93, 96, 102, 105, 111] sc at end of last row)*

Next rows: [Rep rows 4 and 5] 1 [1, 1, 1, 1, 0] time(s). *(90 [96, 99, 105, 108, 111] sc at end of last row)*

CAP SHAPING

Row 1: Ch 1, sk first sc, sl st in each of next 8 sc, ch 1, sk next sc, [3 sc in next sc, sk next 2 sc] 23 [25, 26, 28, 29, 30] times, 2 sc in next sc, sk next sc, sc in next sc, leaving last 8 sc unworked, turn. *(72 [78, 81, 87, 90, 93] sc)*

Row 2: Ch 1, sk first sc, 2 sc in next sc, [sk next 2 sc, 3 sc in next sc] across to last 4 sc, sk next 2 sc, 2 sc in next sc, sk last sc, turn. *(70 [76, 79, 85, 88, 91] sc)*

Row 3: Ch 1, sc in first sc, [sk next 2 sc, 3 sc in next sc] across to last 3 sc, sk next 2 sc, sc in last sc, turn. *(68 [74, 77, 83, 86, 89] sc)*

Row 4: Ch 1, sk first 2 sc, [3 sc in next sc, sk next 2 sc] across to last 3 sc, 2 sc in next sc, sk next sc, sc in last sc, turn. *(66 [72, 75, 81, 84, 87] sc)*

Next rows: [Rep rows 2–4 consecutively] 8 [9, 9, 10, 10, 10] times. At end of last row, fasten off. *(18 [18, 21, 21, 24, 27] sc at end of last row)*

ASSEMBLY

Sew Jacket Fronts to Back at Shoulders.

Fold 1 Sleeve in half lengthwise, place fold at shoulder seam, sew in place.

Rep with rem Sleeve.

Sew side and Sleeve seams.

Sew buttons to Left Front in line with buttonholes on Right Front.

NECKLINE TRIM

On WS of Left Front at neckline, join in first sc, ◊[3 sc in next sc, sk next 2 sc]◊ 2 [3, 3, 4, 4, 5] times, 3 sc in next sc, *now working in ends of rows along shoulder, [3 sc in next row, sk next row] 5 times, 3 sc in last row*, working along back neck edge, sk first sc, rep between ◊ 5 [6, 7, 6, 7, 8] times, 3 sc in next sc, sk last sc, rep between * once, rep between ◊ 3 [4, 4, 5, 5, 6] times, sl st in last sc. Fasten off.

BOTTOM TRIM

On RS of bottom edge of Jacket, working in starting ch on opposite side of row 1, join in first ch of Left Front, 3 sc in same ch, [sk next 2 chs, 3 sc in next ch] across. Fasten off.

SLEEVE TRIM

On RS of bottom edge of Sleeve, working in starting ch on opposite side of row 1, join at seam, ch 1, sk next ch, [3 sc in next ch, sk next 2 chs] around, join in beg sc. Fasten off. ∎

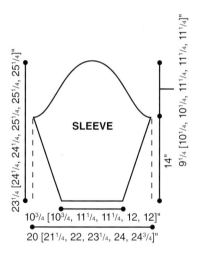

SLEEVE

9¼ [10¼, 10¼, 11¼, 11¼, 11¼]"

14"

23¼ [24¼, 24¼, 25¼, 25¼, 25¼]"

10¾ [10¾, 11¼, 11¼, 12, 12]"

20 [21¼, 22, 23¼, 24, 24¾]"

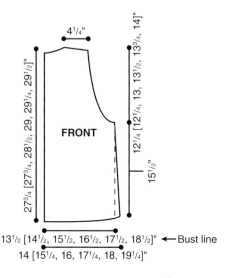

FRONT

4¼"

12¼ [12½, 13, 13½, 13¾, 14]"

15½"

27¾ [27¾, 28½, 29, 29¼, 29½]"

13½ [14½, 15½, 16½, 17½, 18½]" ← Bust line

14 [15¼, 16, 17¼, 18, 19¼]"

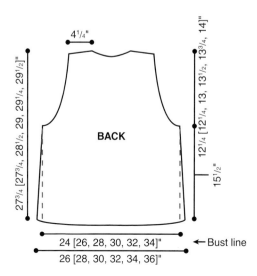

BACK

4¼"

12¼ [12½, 13, 13½, 13¾, 14]"

15½"

27¾ [27¾, 28½, 29, 29¼, 29½]"

24 [26, 28, 30, 32, 34]" ← Bust line

26 [28, 30, 32, 34, 36]"

Soft Shell
TEE

SKILL LEVEL

INTERMEDIATE

FINISHED SIZES

Instructions given fit size X-large; changes for 2X-large, 3X-large, 4X-large, 5X-large and 6X-large are in [ ].

FINISHED GARMENT MEASUREMENTS

Bust: 47 inches (*X-large*) [51 inches (*2X-large*), 55 inches (*3X-large*), 59 inches (*4X-large*), 63 inches (*5X-large*), 67 inches (*6X-large*]

MATERIALS

- NaturallyCaron.com Spa light (light worsted) weight cotton/bamboo yarn (3 oz/251 yds/230g per skein):
  7 [8, 9, 9, 10, 10] skeins #0002 coral lipstick
- Size G/6/4mm crochet hook or size needed to obtain gauge
- Tapestry needle

GAUGE

2 reps of (shell, sc) = 2 inches; 5 pattern rows = 2 inches

Take time to check gauge.

PATTERN NOTES

Back is crocheted first and fastened off. Right Shoulder is crocheted into starting chain of Back and fastened off. Left Shoulder is crocheted into starting chain of Back and joined to Right Shoulder to form Front. Front and Back are then joined and Body is crocheted in rounds.

Chain-3 at beginning of row or round counts as first double crochet unless otherwise stated.

Chain-2 at beginning of Sleeve round counts as double crochet decrease unless otherwise stated.

Join with slip stitch as indicated unless otherwise stated.

SPECIAL STITCHES

Shell: 3 dc in place indicated.

Beginning shell (beg shell): Ch 3 (*see Pattern Notes*), 2 dc in same place.

Decrease (dec): Holding back last lp of each st on hook, 2 dc in place indicated, yo, pull through all lps on hook.

INSTRUCTIONS
TEE
BACK

Row 1 (WS): Ch 98 [98, 98, 110, 110, 110], sc in 2nd ch from hook, [sk next 2 chs, **shell** (see Special Stitches) in next ch, sk next 2 chs, sc in next ch] across, turn. (17 [17, 17, 19, 19, 19] sc, 16 [16, 16, 18, 18, 18] shells)

Row 2 (RS): Ch 3 (see Pattern Notes), dc in same sc, *sk next dc, sc in next dc, sk next dc**, shell in next sc, rep from * across, ending last rep at **, 2 dc in last sc, turn. (16 [16, 16, 18, 18, 18] sc, 4 dc, 15 [15, 15, 17, 17, 17] shells)

Row 3: Ch 1, sc in first dc, [sk next dc, shell in next sc, sk next dc, sc in next dc] across, turn.

Next rows: [Rep rows 2 and 3 alternately] 5 times.

ARMHOLE SHAPING

Row 1: Beg shell (see Pattern Notes) in first sc, [sk next dc, sc in next dc, sk next dc, shell in next sc] across, turn. (16 [16, 16, 18, 18, 18] sc, 17 [17, 17, 19, 19, 19] shells)

Row 2: Beg shell in first dc, *sc in next dc**, sk next dc, shell in next sc, sk next dc, rep from * across, ending last rep at **, shell in last dc, turn. (17 [17, 17, 19, 19, 19] sc, 18 [18, 18, 20, 20, 20] shells)

Next rows: [Rep row 2] 3 [5, 7, 7, 9, 11] times. (20 [22, 24, 26, 28, 30] sc, 21 [23, 25, 27, 29, 31] shells at end of last row)

Next row: Ch 3, dc in same dc, *sc in next dc**, sk next dc, shell in next sc, sk next dc, rep from * across, ending last rep at **, 2 dc in last sc. Fasten off. (21 [23, 25, 27, 29, 31] sc, 4 dc, 20 [22, 24, 26, 28, 30] shells)

RIGHT SHOULDER

Row 1: Working in starting on opposite side of row 1 on RS of Back (WS of first row of Back), **join** (see Pattern Notes) in first ch, sc in same ch, [sk next 2 chs, shell in next ch, sk next 2 chs, sc in next ch] 5 [5, 5, 6, 6, 6] times, leaving rem chs unworked, turn. (6 [6, 6, 7, 7, 7] sc, 5 [5, 5, 6, 6, 6] shells)

Row 2: Ch 1, sk first sc and next dc, sc in next dc, sk next dc, 2 dc in next sc, *sk next dc, sc in next dc, sk next dc**, shell in next sc, rep from * across, ending last rep at **, 2 dc in last sc, turn. (5 [5, 5, 6, 6, 6] sc, 4 dc, 3 [3, 3, 4, 4, 4] shells)

Row 3: Ch 1, sc in first dc, [sk next dc, shell in next sc, sk next dc, sc in next dc] across, leaving last sc unworked, turn. (5 [5, 5, 6, 6, 6] sc, 4 [4, 4, 5, 5, 5] shells)

Row 4: Ch 3, dc in same sc, *sk next dc, sc in next dc, sk next dc**, shell in next sc, rep from * across, ending last rep at **, 2 dc in last sc, turn. (4 [4, 4, 5, 5, 5] sc, 4 dc, 3 [3, 3, 4, 4, 4] shells)

Row 5: Ch 1, sc in first dc, [sk next dc, shell in next sc, sk next dc, sc in next dc] across, turn. (5 [5, 5, 6, 6, 6] sc, 4 [4, 4, 5, 5, 5] shells)

Next rows: [Rep rows 4 and 5 alternately] 7 [5, 5, 5, 5, 3] times.

ARMHOLE SHAPING

Row 1: Beg shell in first sc, *sk next dc, sc in next dc, sk next dc**, shell in next sc, rep from * across, ending last rep at **, 2 dc in last sc, turn. (4 [4, 4, 5, 5, 5] sc, 4 dc, 4 [4, 4, 5, 5, 5] shells)

Row 2: Ch 1, sc in first dc, *sk next dc, shell in next sc, sk next dc, sc in next dc, rep from * across, 2 dc in last dc. Fasten off. (5 [5, 5, 6, 6, 6] sc, 2 dc, 4 [4, 4, 5, 5, 5] shells)

LEFT SHOULDER

Row 1: Working in starting ch on opposite side of row 1 on RS of Back (WS of first row of Back), sk 35 chs from Left Shoulder, join in next ch, sc in same ch, [sk next 2 chs, shell in next ch, sk next 2 chs, sc in next ch] across, turn. (6 [6, 6, 7, 7, 7] sc, 5 [5, 5, 6, 6, 6] shells)

Row 2: Ch 3, dc in same sc, [*sk next dc, sc in next dc, sk next dc*, shell in next sc] 3 [3, 3, 4, 4, 4] times, rep between * once, 2 dc in next sc, rep between * once, leaving last sc unworked, turn. (5 [5, 5, 6, 6, 6] sc, 4 dc, 3 [3, 3, 4, 4, 4] shells)

Row 3: Ch 1, sk first sc, *sc in next dc**, sk next dc, shell in next sc, sk next dc, rep from * across, ending last rep at **, turn. *(5 [5, 5, 6, 6, 6] sc, 4 [4, 4, 5, 5, 5] shells)*

Row 4: Ch 3, dc in same sc, *sk next dc, sc in next dc, sk next dc**, shell in next sc, rep from * across, ending last rep at **, 2 dc in last sc, turn. *(4 [4, 4, 5, 5, 5] sc, 4 dc, 3 [3, 3, 4, 4, 4] shells)*

Row 5: Ch 1, sc in first dc, *sk next dc, shell in next sc, sk next dc, sc in next dc, rep from * across, turn. *(5 [5, 5, 6, 6, 6] sc, 4 [4, 4, 5, 5, 5] shells)*

Next rows: [Rep rows 4 and 5 alternately] 7 [5, 5, 5, 5, 3] times.

ARMHOLE SHAPING

Row 1: Ch 3, dc in same sc, [sk next dc, sc in next dc, sk next dc, shell in next sc] across, turn. *(4 [4, 4, 5, 5, 5] sc, 2 dc, 4 [4, 4, 5, 5, 5] shells)*

Row 2: Ch 3, dc in first dc, *sc in next dc**, sk next dc, shell in next sc, sk next dc, rep from * across, ending last rep at **, turn. *(5 [5, 5, 6, 6, 6] sc, 2 dc, 4 [4, 4, 5, 5, 5] shells)*

FRONT

Row 1: Ch 3, dc in first sc, *sk next dc, sc in next dc**, sk next dc, shell in next sc, rep from * across, ending last rep at **, ch 23, sc in first dc of Right Shoulder, ***sk next dc****, shell in next sc, sk next dc, sc in next dc, rep from *** across, ending last rep at ****, 2 dc in last sc, turn. *(10 [10, 10, 12, 12, 12] sc, 4 dc, 8 [8, 8, 10, 10, 10] shells)*

Row 2: Ch 1, sc in first dc, sk next dc, shell in next sc, [sk next dc, *sc in next dc, sk next dc, shell in next sc*] 4 [4, 4, 5, 5, 5] times, [sk next 2 chs, sc in next ch, ch 4] 6 times, sk next 2 chs, sc in next ch, shell in next sc, sk next dc, rep between * 4 [4, 4, 5, 5, 5] times, sc in last dc, turn. *(17 [17, 17, 19, 19, 19] sc, 10 [10, 10, 12, 12, 12] shells, 6 ch-4 sps)*

Row 3: Ch 3, 2 dc in same sc, *[sk next dc, sc in next dc, sk next dc, shell in next sc] 5 [5, 5, 6, 6, 6] times*, [sc in next ch-4 sp, ch 4] 5 times, sc in next ch-4 sp, shell in next sc, rep between *

once, turn. *(16 [16, 16, 18, 18, 18] sc, 12 [12, 12, 14, 14, 14] shells, 5 ch-4 sps)*

Row 4: Ch 3, dc in same dc, ◊[sc in next dc, sk next dc, *shell in next sc, sk next dc*]◊ 6 [6, 6, 7, 7, 7] times, [sc in next ch-4 sp, ch 4] 4 times, sc in next ch-4 sp, rep between * once, rep between ◊ 5 [5, 5, 6, 6, 6] times, sc in next dc, 2 dc in last dc, turn. *(17 [17, 17, 19, 19, 19] sc, 4 dc, 12 [12, 12, 14, 14, 14] shells, 4 ch-4 sps)*

Row 5: Ch 1, sc in first dc, [*sk next dc, shell in next sc*, sk next dc, sc in next dc] 6 [6, 6, 7, 7, 7] times, rep between * once, [sc in next ch-4 sp, ch 4] 3 times, sc in next ch-4 sp, [shell in next sc, sk next dc, sc in next dc, sk next dc] 7 [7, 7, 8, 8, 8] times, turn. *(18 [18, 18, 20, 20, 20] sc, 14 [14, 14, 16, 16, 16] shells, 3 ch-4 sps)*

Row 6: Ch 3, 2 dc in same dc, *[sk next dc, sc in next dc, sk next dc, shell in next sc] 7 [7, 7, 8, 8, 8] times*, [sc in next ch-4 sp, ch 4] twice, sc in next ch-4 sp, shell in next sc, rep between * once, turn. *(17 [17, 17, 19, 19, 19] sc, 16 [16, 16, 18, 18, 18] shells, 2 ch-4 sps)*

Row 7: Ch 3, 2 dc in same dc, *[sc in next dc, sk next dc, shell in next sc, sk next dc]* 8 [8, 8, 9, 9, 9] times, sc in next ch-4 sp, ch 4, sc in next ch-4 sp, shell in next sc, sk next dc, rep between * 7 [7, 7, 8, 8, 8] times, sc in next dc, shell in last dc, turn. *(18 [18, 18, 20, 20, 20] sc, 18 [18, 18, 20, 20, 20] shells, 1 ch-4 sp)*

Row 8: Ch 3, 2 dc in same dc, ◊[*sc in next dc, sk next dc, shell in next sc*, sk next dc] 8 [8, 8, 9, 9, 9] times◊, rep between * once, sc in next ch-4 sp, shell in next sc, sk next dc, rep between ◊ once, sc in next dc, shell in last dc, turn. *(19 [19, 19, 21, 21, 21] sc, 20 [20, 20, 22, 22, 22] shells)*

Row 9: Ch 3, 2 dc in same dc, *sc in next dc**, sk next dc, shell in next sc, sk next dc, rep from * across, ending last rep at **, shell in last dc, turn. *(20 [20, 20, 22, 22, 22] sc, 21 [21, 21, 23, 23, 23] shells)*

Next rows: Rep last row 0 [2, 4, 4, 6, 8] times. *(20 [22, 24, 26, 28, 30] sc, 21 [23, 25, 27, 29, 31] shells at end of last row)*

BODY

Rnd 1: Now working in rnds, ch 3, dc in first sc, ◊*sc in next dc**, sk next dc, shell in next sc, sk next dc, rep from * across, ending last rep at **◊, 2 dc in last dc, ch 14, now working across Back, rep between ◊ once, ch 14, join in 3rd ch of beg ch-3, turn. *(43 [47, 51, 55, 59, 63] sc, 4 dc, 41 [45, 49, 53, 57, 61] shells)*

Rnd 2: Ch 1, sc in first dc, [sk next 2 chs, shell in next ch, sk next 2 chs, sc in next ch] twice, sk next 2 chs, *shell in next sc**, sk next dc, sc in next dc, sk next dc, rep from * across to next ch, ending last rep at **, [sk next 2 chs, sc in next ch, sk next 2 chs, shell in next ch] twice, sk next 2 chs, ***sc in next dc, sk next dc, shell in next sc, sk next dc, rep from *** around, join in beg sc, turn. *(47 [51, 55, 59, 63, 67] sc, 47 [51, 55, 59, 63, 67] shells)*

Rnd 3: Ch 3, dc in same sc, *sk next dc, sc in next dc, sk next dc**, shell in next sc, rep from * around, ending last rep at **, dc in same sc as first 2 dc, join in 3rd ch of beg ch-3, turn.

Rnd 4: Ch 1, sc in same dc, *sk next dc, shell in next sc, sk next dc**, sc in next dc, rep from * around, ending last rep at **, join in beg sc, turn.

Next rnds: [Rep rnds 3 and 4 alternately] 23 times.

TRIM

Ch 1, sc in each st around, join in beg sc. Fasten off. *(188 [204, 220, 236, 252, 268] sc)*

SLEEVE
MAKE 2.

Row 1 (WS): Beg at cap, ch 26 [32, 26, 32, 26, 32], sc in 2nd ch from hook, [sk next 2 chs, shell in next ch, sk next 2 chs, sc in next ch] across, turn. *(5 [6, 5, 6, 5, 6] sc, 4 [5, 4, 5, 4, 5] shells)*

Row 2: Beg shell in first sc, [sk next dc, sc in next dc, sk next dc, shell in next sc] across, turn. *(4 [5, 4, 5, 4, 5] sc, 5 [6, 5, 6, 5, 6] shells)*

Row 3: Ch 3, 2 dc in same dc, *sc in next dc**, sk next dc, shell in next sc, sk next dc, rep from * across, ending last rep at **, shell in last dc, turn. *(5 [6, 5, 6, 5, 6] sc, 6 [7, 6, 7, 6, 7] shells)*

Next rows: [Rep row 3] 11 [11, 13, 13, 15, 15] times. *(16 [17, 18, 19, 20, 21] sc, 17 [18, 19, 20, 21, 22] shells at end of last row)*

Next row: Ch 3, dc in same dc, *sc in next dc**, sk next dc, shell in next sc, sk next dc, rep from * across, ending last rep at **, 2 dc in last sc, turn. *(17 [18, 19, 20, 21, 22] sc, 4 dc, 16 [17, 18, 19, 20, 21] shells)*

Next row: Ch 1, sc in first dc, [sk next dc, shell in next sc, sk next dc, sc in next dc] across, turn. *(18 [19, 20, 21, 22, 23] sc, 17 [18, 19, 20, 21, 22] shells)*

BODY

Rnd 1: Ch 3, dc in same sc, sk next dc, *sc in next dc, sk next dc**, shell in next sc, sk next dc, rep from * across, ending last rep at **, 2 dc in last sc, ch 17, join in 3rd ch of beg ch-3, turn. *(17 [18, 19, 20, 21, 22] sc, 4 dc, 16 [17, 18, 19, 20, 21] shells)*

Rnd 2: Ch 1, sc in first dc, ◊[sk next 2 chs, shell in next ch, sk next 2 chs◊, sc in next ch] twice, rep between ◊ once, [sc in next dc, sk next dc, shell in next sc, sk next dc] around, join in beg sc, turn. *(20 [21, 22, 23, 24, 25] sc, 20 [21, 22, 23, 24, 25] shells)*

Rnd 3: Ch 3, dc in same dc, *sk next dc, sc in next dc, sk next dc**, shell in next sc, rep from * around, ending last rep at **, dc in same st as beg ch-3, join in 3rd ch of beg ch-3, turn.

Rnd 4: Ch 1, sc in first dc, *sk next dc, shell in next sc, sk next dc**, sc in next dc, rep from * around, ending last rep at **, join in beg sc, turn.

Rnds 5 & 6: Rep rnds 3 and 4.

Rnd 7: Ch 3, dc in same sc, *[sk next dc, sc in next dc, sk next dc*, shell in next sc] 17 [18, 19, 20, 21, 22] times, rep between * once, [**dec** *(see Special Stitches)* in next sc *(dec is counted and used as dc)*, sk next dc, sc in next dc, sk next dc] twice, dc in same st as beg ch-3, join in 3rd ch of beg ch-3, turn. *(20 [21, 22, 23, 24, 25] sc, 2 dc, 18 [19, 20, 21, 22, 23] shells)*

Rnd 8: Ch 1, sc in first dc, sk next dc, shell in next sc, sk next dc, sc in next sc, *sk next dc, shell in next sc, sk next dc**, sc in next dc, rep from * around, ending last rep at **, join in beg sc, turn. *(19 [20, 21, 22, 23, 24] sc, 19 [20, 21, 22, 23, 24] shells)*

Rnd 9: Rep rnd 3.

Rnd 10: Ch 1, sc in first dc, [sk next dc, dec in next sc, sk next dc, sc in next dc] twice, *sk next dc, shell in next sc, sk next dc**, sc in next dc, rep from * around, ending last rep at **, join in 3rd ch of beg ch-3, turn. *(19 [20, 21, 22, 23, 24] sc, 2 dc, 17 [18, 19, 20, 21, 22] shells)*

Rnd 11: Ch 3, dc in same sc, [sk next dc, sc in next sc, sk next dc, shell in next sc] 17 [18, 19, 20, 21, 22] times, sk next dc, sc in next sc, sk next dc, dc in same st as beg ch-3, join in 3rd ch of beg ch-3, turn. *(18 [19, 20, 21, 22, 23] sc, 18 [19, 20, 21, 22, 23] shells)*

Rnd 12: Rep rnd 4.

Rnd 13: Ch 2 *(see Pattern Notes)*, dc in first sc, *[sk next dc, sc in next dc, sk next dc*, shell in next sc] 16 [17, 18, 19, 20, 21] times, rep between * once, dec in next sc, sk next dc, sc in next dc, join in first dc, turn. *(18 [19, 20, 21, 22, 23] sc, 2 dc, 16 [17, 18, 19, 20, 21] shells)*

Rnd 14: Ch 1, sl st in next sc, ch 1, sc in same sc, *sk next dc, shell in next sc, sk next dc**, sc in next sc, rep from * around, ending last rep at **, join in beg sc, turn. *(17 [18, 19, 20, 21, 22] sc, 17 [18, 19, 20, 21, 22] shells)*

Rnd 15: Rep rnd 3.

Rnd 16: Ch 1, sc in first dc, sk next dc, dec in next sc, *[sk next dc, sc in next dc, sk next dc*, shell in next sc] 15 times, rep between * once, dec in next sc, join in beg sc, turn. *(17 [18, 19, 20, 21, 22] sc, 2 dc, 15 [16, 17, 18, 19, 20] shells)*

Rnd 17: Ch 1, sc in first sc, *sk next dc, shell in next sc, sk next dc**, sc in next sc, rep from * around, ending last rep at **, join in beg sc, turn. *(16 [17, 18, 19, 20, 21] sc, 16 [17, 18, 19, 20, 21] shells)*

Rnds 18 & 19: Rep rnds 3 and 4.

TRIM

Ch 1, sc in each st around, join in beg sc. Fasten off. *(64 [68, 72, 76, 80, 84] sc)*

ASSEMBLY

Matching underarm centers and easing to fit, sew Sleeves into armholes.

FINISHING
NECKLINE TRIM

With RS facing, join in first ch sp on neck edge of Back, 3 sc in each ch sp across to Left Shoulder, now working in ends of rows, evenly sp sc across to Front, 3 sc in each ch sp across to Right Shoulder, again working in ends of rows, evenly sp sc across to Back, join in beg sc. Fasten off. ∎

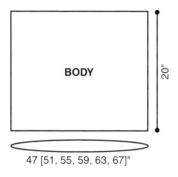

BODY

20"

47 [51, 55, 59, 63, 67]"

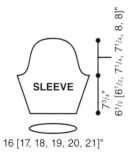

SLEEVE

7¾"

6½ [6½, 7¼, 7¼, 8, 8]"

16 [17, 18, 19, 20, 21]"

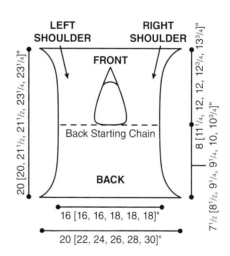

LEFT SHOULDER   RIGHT SHOULDER

FRONT

Back Starting Chain

BACK

20 [20, 21½, 21½, 23¼, 23¼]"

8 [11¼, 12, 12, 12¾, 13¾]"

7½ [8½, 9¼, 9¼, 10, 10¾]"

16 [16, 16, 18, 18, 18]"

20 [22, 24, 26, 28, 30]"

Lightning Shell
JACKET

SKILL LEVEL

INTERMEDIATE

FINISHED SIZES

Instructions given fit size X-large; changes for 2X-large, 3X-large, 4X-large, 5X-large and 6X-large are in [ ].

FINISHED GARMENT MEASUREMENTS

Bust: 48 inches *(X-large)* [51½ inches *(2X-large)*, 55 inches *(3X-large)*, 58¾ inches *(4X-large)*, 64 inches *(5X-large)*, 69¼ inches *(6X-large]*

MATERIALS

- Classic Elite Cotton Bam Boo light (light worsted) weight cotton/bamboo yarn (1¾ oz/130 yds/ 50g per ball):
    17 [19, 21, 23, 24, 26] balls
    #3638 toasted almond
    1 [1, 1, 1, 1, 1] ball #3636 sesame
- Size G/6/4mm crochet hook or size needed to obtain gauge
- Tapestry needle
- Sewing needle
- Sewing thread
- ¾-inch buttons: 5

GAUGE

9 shells = 8 inches; 9 shell rows = 3 inches

Take time to check gauge.

PATTERN NOTES

A-line body of Jacket is crocheted first in 1 piece. Fronts and Back are then crocheted from body up and joined at shoulders.

Use toasted almond throughout unless otherwise stated.

Chain-3 at beginning of row or round counts as first double crochet unless otherwise stated.

Chain-4 at beginning of row or round counts as first double crochet and chain-1 unless otherwise stated.

Join with slip stitch as indicated unless otherwise stated.

SPECIAL STITCHES

Shell: (Sc, ch 3, 3 dc) in place indicated.

V-stitch (V-st): (Dc, ch 1, dc) in place indicated.

Beginning V-stitch (beg V-st): Ch 4 *(see Pattern Notes)*, dc in same place.

INSTRUCTIONS
JACKET
BODY

Row 1 (WS): With **toasted almond** *(see Pattern Notes)*, ch 234 [250, 266, 282, 306, 330], **shell** *(see Special Stitches)* in 2nd ch from hook, sk next 3 chs, [shell in next ch, sk next 3 chs] across, sc in last ch, turn. *(1 sc, 58 [62, 66, 70, 76, 82] shells)*

Row 2: Ch 3 *(see Pattern Notes)*, dc in same sc, *sk next 3 dc, sc in next ch-3**, **V-st** *(see Special Stitches)* in next sc, rep from * across, ending last rep at **, dc in last sc, turn. *(3 dc, 58 [62, 66, 70, 76, 82] sc, 57 [61, 65, 69, 75, 81] V-sts)*

Row 3: Ch 3, shell in next sc, [sk next V-st, shell in next sc] across, sl st in last dc, turn. *(1 dc, 58 [62, 66, 70, 76, 82] shells)*

Row 4: Ch 3, *sk next 3 dc, sc in next ch-3**, V-st in next sc, rep from * across, ending last rep at **, dc in next sc, dc in last dc, turn. *(3 dc, 58 [62, 66, 70, 76, 82] sc, 57 [61, 65, 69, 75, 81] V-sts)*

Row 5: Ch 3, dc in same dc, sk next dc, [shell in next sc, sk next V-st] across, (sc, dc) in next sc, dc in last dc, turn. *(1 sc, 4 dc, 57 [61, 65, 69, 75, 81] shells)*

Row 6: Ch 1, sc in first dc, sk next dc, *V-st in next sc**, sk next 3 dc, sc in next ch-3, rep from * across, ending last rep at **, sk next dc, sc in last dc, turn. *(59 [63, 67, 71, 77, 79] sc, 58 [62, 66, 70, 76, 82] V-sts)*

Row 7: Ch 1, [shell in next sc, sk next V-st] across, sc in last sc, turn. *(1 sc, 58 [62, 66, 70, 76, 82] shells)*

Rows 8–13: Rep rows 2–7.

Rows 14 & 15: Rep rows 2 and 3.

Row 16: Ch 3, ◊[sk next 3 dc, sc in next ch-3, V-st in next sc]◊ 13 [14, 15, 16, 18, 20] times, *[sk next 3 dc, sc in next ch-3, dc in next sc] twice*, rep between ◊ 27 [29, 31, 33, 35, 37] times, rep between * once, rep between ◊ 13 [14, 15, 16, 18, 20] times, sk next 3 dc, sc in next ch-3, dc in next sc, dc in last dc, turn. *(7 dc, 58 [62, 66, 70, 76, 82] sc, 53 [57, 61, 65, 71, 77] V-sts)*

Row 17: Ch 3, dc in same dc, sk next dc, ◊[shell in next sc, sk next V-st]◊ 13 [14, 15, 16, 18, 20] times, *shell in next sc, sk next dc and next sc, **sc dec** *(see Stitch Guide)* in next dc and next sc, ch 3, 3 dc in same sc, sk next V-st*, rep between ◊ 26 [28, 30, 32, 34, 36] times, rep between * once, rep between ◊ 12 [13, 14, 15, 17, 19] times, (sc, dc) in next sc, dc in last dc, turn. *(1 sc, 4 dc, 57 [61, 65, 69, 75, 81] shells)*

Rows 18 & 19: Rep rows 6 and 7. *(1 sc, 56 [60, 64, 68, 74, 80] shells at end of last row)*

Rows 20–31: [Rep rows 2–7 consecutively] twice.

Row 32: Ch 3, dc in same sc, ◊[sk next 3 dc, sc in next ch-3, V-st in next sc]◊ 12 [13, 14, 15, 17, 19] times, *[sk next 3 dc, sc in next ch-3, dc in next sc] twice*, rep between ◊ 27 [29, 31, 33, 35, 37] times, rep between * once, rep between ◊ 12 [13, 14, 15, 17, 19] times, sk next 3 dc, sc in next ch-3, dc in last dc, turn. *(7 dc, 54 [58, 62, 66, 72, 78] sc, 49 [53, 57, 61, 67, 73] V-sts)*

Row 33: Ch 3, ◊[shell in next sc, sk next V-st]◊ 12 [13, 14, 15, 17, 19] times, *shell in next sc, sk next dc and next sc, sc dec in next dc and next sc, ch 3, 3 dc in same sc, sk next V-st*, rep between ◊ 26 [28, 30, 32, 34, 36] times, rep between * once, rep between ◊ 12 [13, 14, 15, 17, 19] times, sl st in last dc, turn. *(1 dc, 54 [58, 62, 66, 72, 78] shells)*

Rows 34–37: Rep rows 4–7. *(1 sc, 54 [58, 62, 66, 72, 78] shells at end of last row)*

Rows 38–43: Rep rows 2–7.

Rows 44–48: Rep rows 2–6. *(55 [59, 63, 67, 73, 78] sc, 54 [58, 62, 66, 72, 78] V-sts at end of last row)*

LEFT FRONT

Row 1: Ch 1, shell in first sc, sk next V-st, [shell in next sc, sk next V-st] 11 [11, 13, 13, 14, 14] times, sc in next sc, leaving rem sts unworked, turn. *(1 sc, 12 [12, 14, 14, 15, 15] shells)*

Row 2: Ch 3, *sk next 3 dc, sc in next ch-3**, V-st in next sc, rep from * across, ending last rep at **, dc in last sc, turn. *(12 [12, 14, 14, 15, 15] sc, 2 dc, 11 [11, 13, 13, 14, 14] V-sts)*

Row 3: Ch 3, [shell in next sc, sk next V-st] across, sc in last sc, turn. *(1 sc, 1 dc, 11 [11, 13, 13, 14, 14] shells)*

Row 4: Ch 3, *sk next 3 dc, sc in next ch-3**, V-st in next sc, rep from * across, ending last rep at **, dc in each of last 2 dc, turn. *(3 dc, 11 [11, 13, 13, 14, 14] sc, 10 [10, 12, 12, 13, 13] V-sts)*

Row 5: Ch 3, dc in same dc, sk next dc, [shell in next sc, sk next V-st] across, sc in next sc, leaving last dc unworked, turn. *(1 sc, 2 dc, 10 [10, 12, 12, 13, 13] shells)*

Row 6: Ch 3, [sk next 3 dc, sc in next ch-3, V-st in next sc] across, sk next dc, sc in last dc, turn. *(1 dc, 11 [11, 13, 13, 14, 14] sc, 10 [10, 12, 12, 13, 13] V-sts)*

Row 7: Ch 1, [shell in next sc, sk next V-st] across, sc in last sc, turn. *(1 sc, 10 [10, 12, 12, 13, 13] shells)*

Next rows: [Rep rows 2–7] 0 [0, 1, 1, 1, 1] time(s). *(1 sc, 10 [10, 10, 10, 11, 11] shells at end of last row)*

BODICE

Row 1: Ch 3, dc in same sc, *sk next 3 dc, sc in next ch-3**, V-st in next sc, rep from * across, ending last rep at **, dc in last sc, turn. *(3 dc, 10 [10, 10, 10, 11, 11] sc, 9 [9, 11, 11, 12, 12] V-sts)*

Row 2: Ch 3, [shell in next sc, sk next V-st] across, sl st in last dc, turn. *(1 dc, 10 [10, 10, 10, 11, 11] shells)*

Row 3: Ch 3, *sk next 3 dc, sc in next ch-3**, V-st in next sc, rep from * across, ending last rep at **, dc in next sc, dc in last dc, turn. *(3 dc, 9 [9, 9, 9, 10, 10] V-sts, 10 [10, 10, 10, 11, 11] sc)*

Row 4: Ch 3, dc in same dc, sk next dc, [shell in next sc, sk next V-st] across, (sc, dc) in next sc, dc in last dc, turn. *(1 sc, 4 dc, 9 [9, 9, 9, 10, 10] shells)*

Row 5: Ch 1, sc in first dc, sk next dc, *V-st in next sc**, sk next 3 dc, sc in next ch-3, rep from * across, ending last rep at **, sk next dc, sc in last dc, turn. *(11 [11, 11, 11, 12, 12] sc, 10 [10, 10, 10, 11, 11] V-sts)*

Row 6: Ch 1, shell in first sc, sk next V-st, [shell in next sc, sk next V-st] across, sc in last sc, turn. *(1 sc, 10 [10, 10, 10, 11, 11] shells)*

Next rows: [Rep rows 1–6 of Bodice consecutively] twice.

Next row: Rep row 1 of Bodice.

NECKLINE SHAPING

Row 1: Ch 1, [sl st in next dc, sl st in next sc and in next dc, sk next ch-1 sp] 3 [3, 3, 3, 4, 4] times, sl st in next dc, ch 1, [shell in next sc, sk next V-st] across, sl st in last dc, turn. *(7 shells)*

Row 2: Ch 3, *sk next 3 dc, sc in next ch-3**, V-st in next sc, rep from * across, ending last rep at **, leaving last sc unworked, turn. *(1 dc, 6 V-sts, 7 sc)*

Row 3: Ch 1, shell in first sc, sk next V-st, [shell in next sc, sk next V-st] across, (sc, dc) in next sc, dc in last dc, turn. *(1 sc, 2 dc, 6 shells)*

Row 4: Ch 1, sc in first dc, sk next dc, [V-st in next sc, sk next 3 dc, sc in next ch-3] across, turn. *(7 sc, 6 V-sts)*

Row 5: Ch 1, [shell in next sc, sk next V-st] across, sc in last sc, turn. *(1 sc, 6 shells)*

Row 6: Ch 3, dc in same sc, *sk next 3 dc, sc in next ch-3**, V-st in next sc, rep from * across, ending last rep at **, dc in last dc, turn. *(6 sc, 3 dc, 5 V-sts)*

Row 7: Ch 3, [shell in next sc, sk next V-st] across, sl st in last dc, turn. *(1 dc, 6 shells)*

Row 8: Ch 3, *sk next 3 dc, sc in next ch-3**, V-st in next sc, rep from * across, ending last rep at **, dc in next sc, dc in last dc, turn. *(6 sc, 3 dc, 5 V-sts)*

Row 9: Ch 3, dc in same dc, sk next dc, [shell in next sc, sk next V-st] across, (sc, dc) in next sc, dc in last dc, turn. *(1 sc, 4 dc, 5 shells)*

Row 10: Ch 1, sc in first dc, sk next dc, *V-st in next sc**, sk next 3 dc, sc in next ch-3, rep from * across, ending last rep at **, sk next dc, sc in last dc, turn. Fasten off. *(7 sc, 6 V-sts)*

BACK

Row 1: With WS facing, sk next 3 [5, 5, 7, 8, 11] V-sts on last row of Body, **join** *(see Pattern Notes)* in next sc, shell in same sc, sk next V-st, [shell in next sc, sk next V-st] 23 [23, 25, 25, 27, 27] times, sc in next sc, leaving rem sts unworked, turn. *(1 sc, 24 [24, 26, 26, 28, 28] shells)*

Row 2: Ch 3, *sk next 3 dc, sc in next ch-3**, V-st in next sc, rep from * across, ending last rep at **, leaving last sc unworked, turn. *(1 dc, 24 [24, 26, 26, 28, 28] sc, 23 [23, 25, 25, 27, 27] V-sts)*

Row 3: Ch 1, shell in first sc, sk next V-st, [shell in next sc, sk next V-st] across, sc in last sc, turn. *(1 sc, 23 [23, 25, 25, 27, 27] shells)*

Next rows: [Rep rows 2 and 3 alternately] 4 [4, 5, 5, 6, 6] times. *(1 sc, 19 [19, 20, 20, 21, 21] shells at end of last row)*

BODICE

Row 1: Ch 3, dc in same sc, *sk next 3 dc, sc in next ch-3**, V-st in next sc, rep from * across, ending last rep at **, dc in last sc, turn. *(3 dc, 19 [19, 20, 20, 21, 21] sc, 18 [18, 19, 19, 20, 20] V-sts)*

Row 2: Ch 3, [shell in next sc, sk next V-st] across, sl st in last dc, turn. *(1 dc, 19 [19, 20, 20, 21, 21] shells)*

Row 3: Ch 3, *sk next 3 dc, sc in next ch-3**, V-st in next sc, rep from * across, ending last rep at **, dc in next sc, dc in last dc, turn. *(3 dc, 19 [19, 20, 20, 21, 21] sc, 18 [18, 19, 19, 20, 20] V-sts)*

Row 4: Ch 3, dc in same dc, sk next dc, [shell in next sc, sk next V-st] across, (sc, dc) in next sc, dc in last dc, turn. *(1 sc, 4 dc, 18 [18, 19, 19, 20, 20] shells)*

Row 5: Ch 1, sc in first dc, sk next dc, *V-st in next sc**, sk next 3 dc, sc in next ch-3, rep from * across, ending last rep at **, sk next dc, sc in last dc, turn. *(20 [20, 21, 21, 22, 22] sc, 19 [19, 20, 20, 21, 21] V-sts)*

Row 6: Ch 1, [shell in next sc, sk next V-st] across, sc in last sc, turn. *(1 sc, 19 [19, 20, 20, 21, 21] shells)*

Next rows: [Rep rows 1–6 consecutively] twice.

Next rows: [Rep rows 1–5] once. At end of last row, fasten off.

RIGHT FRONT

Row 1: With WS facing, sk next 3 [5, 5, 7, 8, 11] V-sts on last row of Body, join in next sc, ch 1, shell in same sc, *sk next V-st**, shell in next sc, rep from * across, ending last rep at **, sc in last sc, turn. *(1 sc, 12 [12, 14, 14, 15, 15] shells)*

Row 2: Ch 3, dc in same sc, *sk next 3 dc, sc in next ch-3**, V-st in next sc, rep from * across, ending last rep at **, leaving last sc unworked, turn. *(2 dc, 12 [12, 14, 14, 15, 15] sc, 11 [11, 13, 13, 14, 14] V-sts)*

Row 3: Ch 3, dc in same sc, [sk next V-st, shell in next sc] across, sl st in last dc, turn. *(2 dc, 11 [11, 13, 13, 14, 14] shells)*

Row 4: Ch 3, *sk next 3 dc, sc in next ch-3**, V-st in next sc, rep from * across, ending last rep at **, dc in next sc, sk next dc, dc in last dc, turn. *(3 dc, 11 [11, 13, 13, 14, 14] sc, 10 [10, 12, 12, 13, 13] V-sts)*

Row 5: Ch 3, sk next dc, [shell in next sc, sk next V-st] across, (sc, dc) in next sc, dc in last dc, turn. *(1 sc, 3 dc, 10 [10, 12, 12, 13, 13] shells)*

Row 6: Ch 1, sc in first dc, sk next dc, [V-st in next sc, sk next 3 dc, sc in next ch-3] across, dc in next sc, leaving last dc unworked, turn. *(1 dc, 11 [11, 13, 13, 14, 14] sc, 110 [10, 12, 12, 13, 13] V-sts)*

Row 7: Ch 1, sk first dc, [shell in next sc, sk next V-st] across, sc in last sc, turn. *(1 sc, 10 [10, 12, 12, 13, 13] shells)*

BODICE
Work same as for Bodice on Left Front.

NECKLINE SHAPING
Row 1: Ch 3, [shell in next sc, sk next V-st] 6 times, (sc, dc) in next sc, dc in next dc, leaving rem sts unworked, turn. *(1 sc, 3 dc, 6 shells)*

Row 2: Ch 1, sc in first dc, sk next dc, [V-st in next sc, sk next dc, sc in next ch-3] across, dc in next sc, dc in last dc, turn. *(7 sc, 2 dc, 6 V-sts)*

Row 3: Ch 3, dc in same dc, sk next dc, [shell in next sc, sk next V-st] across, sl st in last sc, turn. *(2 dc, 6 shells)*

Row 4: Ch 3, [sk next 3 dc, sc in next ch-3, V-st in next sc] across, sc in last dc, turn. *(7 sc, 1 dc, 6 V-sts)*

Row 5: Ch 1, shell in first sc, sk next V-st, [shell in next sc, sk next V-st] across, sc in last sc, turn. *(1 sc, 6 shells)*

Row 6: Ch 3, dc in same sc, *sk next 3 dc, sc in next ch-3**, V-st in next sc, rep from * across, ending last rep at **, dc in last sc, turn. *(3 dc, 6 sc, 5 V-sts)*

Row 7: Ch 3, [shell in next sc, sk next V-st] across, sl st in last dc, turn. *(1 dc, 6 shells)*

Row 8: Ch 3, *sk next 3 dc, sc in next ch-3**, V-st in next sc, rep from * across, ending last rep at **, dc in next sc, dc in last sc, turn. *(3 dc, 6 sc, 5 V-sts)*

Row 9: Ch 3, dc in same dc, sk next dc, [shell in next sc, sk next V-st] across, (sc, dc) in next sc, dc in last dc, turn. *(1 sc, 4 dc, 5 shells)*

Row 10: Ch 1, sc in first dc, sk next dc, *V-st in next sc**, sk next 3 dc, sc in next ch-3, rep from * across, ending last rep at **, sk next dc, sc in last dc, turn. *(7 sc, 6 V-sts)*

JOINING FRONT TO BACK
RIGHT SHOULDER
Working along WS of Right Shoulder and slip stitching along RS of Back, ch 1, *sc in next sc of Shoulder, ch 2, sl st in next sc of Back, 2 dc in same sc of Shoulder, sl st in ch-1 sp of next V-st of Back, dc in same sc of Shoulder**, sk next V-st of Shoulder, rep from * across, ending last rep at **, sl st in next sc of Back. Fasten off. *(1 sc, 6 shells)*

LEFT SHOULDER
Working along WS of Left Shoulder and slip stitching along RS of Back, sk next 5 [5, 6, 6, 7, 7] V-sts of Back, join in next ch-1 sp of Back, ch 2, sc in first sc of Shoulder, *ch 2, sl st in next sc of Back**, 2 dc in same sc of Shoulder, sl st in next ch-1 sp of Back, dc in same sc of Shoulder, sk next V-st of Shoulder, sc in next sc of Shoulder, rep from * across, ending last rep at **. Fasten off. *(1 sc, 6 shells)*

SLEEVE
MAKE 2.
Rnd 1 (WS): Ch 64 [72, 72, 80, 80, 88], taking care not to twist chain, sl st in first ch to form ring, ch 1, [shell in next ch, sk next 3 chs] around, join in beg sc, **turn.** *(16 [18, 18, 20, 20, 22] shells)*

Rnd 2 (RS): **Beg V-st** *(see Special Stitches)* in first sc, [sk next 3 dc, sc in next ch-3, dc in next sc] twice, *sk next 3 dc, sc in next ch-3**, V-st in next sc, rep from * around, ending last rep at **, join in 3rd ch of beg ch-4, turn. *(2 dc, 16 [18, 18, 20, 20, 22] sc, 14 [16, 16, 18, 18, 20] V-sts)*

Rnd 3: Ch 1, [shell in next sc, sk next V-st] 13 [15, 15, 17, 17, 19] times, shell in next sc, sk next dc and next sc, sc dec in next dc and next sc, ch 3, 3 dc in same sc, sk next V-st, join in beg sc, turn. *(15 [17, 17, 19, 19, 21] shells)*

Rnd 4: Beg V-st in first sc, *sk next 3 dc, sc in next ch-3**, V-st in next sc, rep from * around, ending last rep at **, join in 3rd ch of beg ch-4, turn. *(15 [17, 17, 19, 19, 21] sc, 15 [17, 17, 19, 19, 21] V-sts)*

Rnd 5: Ch 1, [shell in next sc, sk next V-st] around, join in beg sc, turn.

Rnd 6: Beg V-st in first sc, [sk next 3 dc, sc in next ch-3, dc in next sc] twice, *sk next 3 dc, sc in next ch-3**, V-st in next sc, rep from * around, ending last rep at **, join in 3rd ch of beg ch-4, turn. *(2 dc, 15 [17, 17, 19, 19, 21] sc, 13 [15, 15, 17, 17, 19] V-sts)*

Rnd 7: Ch 1, [shell in next sc, sk next V-st] 13 [15, 15, 17, 17, 19] times, shell in next sc, sk next dc and next sc, sc dec in next dc and next sc, ch 3, 3 dc in same sc, sk next V-st, join in beg sc, turn. *(14 [16, 16, 18, 18, 20] shells)*

Rnd 8: Beg V-st in first sc, *sk next 3 dc, sc in next ch-3**, V-st in next sc, rep from * around, ending last rep at **, join in 3rd ch of beg ch-4, turn. *(15 [17, 17, 19, 19, 21] sc, (15 [17, 17, 19, 19, 21] V-sts)*

Rnd 9: Ch 1, [shell in next sc, sk next V-st] around, join in beg sc, turn.

Rnds 10–15: [Rep rnds 8 and 9 alternately] 3 times.

Rnd 16: Beg V-st in first sc, *sc in next ch-3, V-st in next sc, rep from * around to last sc, (V-st, ch 1, dc) in last sc, sc in next ch-3, join in 3rd ch of beg ch-4, turn. *(14 [16, 16, 18, 18, 20] sc, (15 [17, 17, 19, 19, 21] V-sts)*

Rnd 17: Ch 1, shell in first sc, sk next ch-1, shell in next dc, sk next ch-1 and next dc, *shell in next sc, sk next V-st, rep from * around, join in beg sc, turn. *(15 [17, 17, 19, 19, 21] shells)*

Rnds 18–21: [Rep rnds 8 and 9 alternately] twice.

Rnds 22–45: [Rep rnds 16–23 consecutively] 4 times. *(19 [21, 21, 23, 23, 25] shells at end of last rnd)*

Rnds 46 & 47: Rep rnds 16 and 17. *(20 [22, 22, 24, 24, 26] shells at end of last rnd)*

Rnd 48: Rep rnd 8. *(20 [22, 22, 24, 24, 26] sc, 20 [22, 22, 24, 24, 26] V-sts)*

CAP SHAPING
Row 1: Now working in rows, ch 1, [shell in next sc, sk next V-st] 16 [18, 18, 20, 20, 22] times, sc in next sc, leaving rem sts unworked, turn. *(16 [18, 18, 20, 20, 22] shells)*

Row 2: Ch 3, *sk next 3 dc, sc in next ch-3**, V-st in next sc, rep from * across, ending last rep at **, leaving last sc unworked, turn. *(16 [18, 18, 20, 20, 22] sc, 15 [17, 17, 19, 19, 21] V-sts)*

Row 3: Ch 3, 2 dc in same sc, sk next V-st, *shell in next sc, sk next V-st, rep from * across, sc in last sc, turn. *(3 dc, 14 [16, 16, 18, 18, 20] shells)*

Next rows: [Rep rows 2 and 3 alternately] 8 [9, 10, 11, 12, 13] times. *(3 dc, 7 [8, 7, 8, 7, 8] shells at end of last row)*

Next row: Rep row 2. Fasten off. *(8 [9, 8, 9, 8, 9] sc, 7 [8, 7, 8, 7, 8] V-sts)*

ASSEMBLY

Matching underarm centers and easing to fit, sew Sleeves into armholes.

SLEEVE TRIM

Rnd 1: With WS facing and working in starting ch on opposite side of rnd 1, join in ch-3 sp, shell in each ch-3 sp around, **changing colors** *(see Stitch Guide)* to sesame in last st, join in beg sc, **turn**. *(16 [18, 18, 20, 20, 22] shells)*

Rnd 2: Beg V-st in first sc, *sk next 3 dc, sc in next ch-3**, V-st in next sc, rep from * around, ending last rep at **, changing to toasted almond in last st, join in 3rd ch of beg ch-4, turn. *(16 [18, 18, 20, 20, 22] sc, (16 [18, 18, 20, 20, 22] V-sts)*

Rnd 3: Ch 1, [shell in next sc, sk next V-st] around, join in beg sc. Fasten off.

JACKET TRIM

Rnd 1: With WS facing and working in starting ch on opposite side of row 1, with toasted almond, join in first ch-3 sp, shell in same ch sp, shell in each ch-3 sp across, working in ends of rows, sk rows as needed, evenly sp shells around to Right Front, shell once, [ch 1 *(buttonhole)*, shell 4 times] 5 times, shell evenly along rem of Right Front, changing to sesame in last st, join in beg sc, **turn.**

Rnd 2: Beg V-st in first sc, *sk next 3 dc, sc in next ch-3**, V-st in next sc, working V-st in ch-1 sps for buttonholes, rep from * around, ending last rep at **, changing to toasted almond in last st, join in 3rd ch of beg ch-4, turn.

Rnd 3: Ch 1, [shell in next sc, sk next V-st] around, join in beg sc. Fasten off.

FINISHING

Sew buttons to Left Front opposite buttonholes on Right Front. ∎

SLEEVE

16" 6½ [7¼, 8, 8½, 9½, 10]"

14¼ [16, 16, 17¾, 17¾, 19½]"

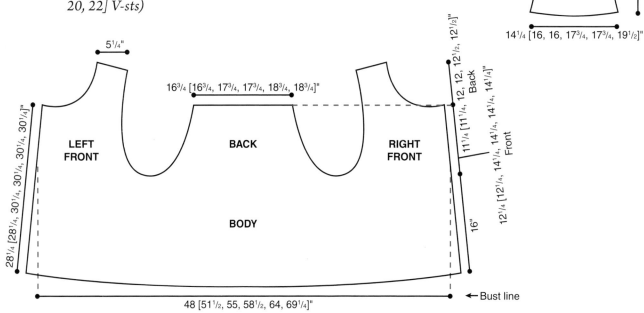

5¼"

16¾ [16¾, 17¾, 17¾, 18¾, 18¾]"

11¼ [11¼, 12, 12, 12½, 12½]"
Back

12¼ [12¼, 14¼, 14¼, 14¼, 14¼]"
Front

28¼ [28¼, 30¼, 30¼, 30¼, 30¼]"

LEFT FRONT   BACK   RIGHT FRONT

16"

BODY

← Bust line

48 [51½, 55, 58½, 64, 69¼]"

← Bottom edge

51½ [55, 58½, 62¼, 67½, 72¾]"

Shell of SHELLS

FINISHED SIZES

Instructions given fit size X-large; changes for 2X-large, 3X-large, 4X-large, 5X-large and 6X-large are in [ ].

FINISHED GARMENT MEASUREMENTS

Bust: 44½ inches *(X-large)* [48 inches *(2X-large)*, 53¼ inches *(3X-large)*, 56¾ inches *(4X-large)*, 62¼ inches *(5X-large)*, 65¾ inches *(6X-large]*

MATERIALS

- Classic Elite Cotton Bam Boo light (light worsted) weight cotton/ bamboo yarn (1¾ oz/130 yds/ 50g per ball):
  9 [9, 10, 11, 11, 12] balls #3636 sesame
- Size G/6/4mm crochet hook or size needed to obtain gauge
- Tapestry needle

GAUGE

9 shells = 8 inches; 9 shell rows = 3 inches

Take time to check gauge.

PATTERN NOTES

Shell is very close fitting.

Body of Shell is crocheted first in rounds. Front and Back Bodice are then crocheted from the Body up and joined at shoulders.

Chain-3 at beginning of row or round counts as first double crochet unless otherwise stated.

Chain-4 at beginning of row or round counts as first double crochet and chain-1 unless otherwise stated.

Join with slip stitch as indicated unless otherwise stated.

SPECIAL STITCHES

Shell: (Sc, ch 3, 3 dc) in place indicated.

V-stitch (V-st): (Dc, ch 1, dc) in place indicated.

Beginning V-stitch (beg V-st): Ch 4 *(see Pattern Notes)*, dc in same place.

INSTRUCTIONS

SHELL
BODY

Rnd 1 (WS): Ch 200 [216, 240, 256, 280, 296], taking care not to twist chain, sl st in first ch to form circle, ch 1, **shell** *(see Special Stitches)* in first ch, sk next 3 chs, [shell in next ch, sk next 3 chs] around, **join** *(see Pattern Notes)* in beg sc, turn. *(50 [54, 60, 64, 70, 74] shells)*

Rnd 2 (RS): **Beg V-st** (*see Special Stitches*), *sk next 3 dc, sc in next ch-3**, **V-st** (*see Special Stitches*) in next sc, rep from * around, ending last rep at **, join in 3rd ch of beg ch-4, turn. (*50 [54, 60, 64, 70, 74] sc, 50 [54, 60, 64, 70, 72] V-sts*)

Rnd 3: Ch 1, shell in first sc, sk next V-st, [shell in next sc, sk next V-st] around, turn.

Rnds 4–43: [Rep rnds 2 and 3 alternately] 20 times.

Rnd 44: Rep rnd 2.

BACK

Row 1: Ch 1, shell in first sc, sk next V-st, [shell in next sc, sk next V-st] 19 [19, 22, 22, 25, 25] times, sc in next sc, leaving rem sts unworked, turn. (*1 sc, 20 [20, 23, 23, 26, 26] shells*)

Row 2: Ch 3 (*see Pattern Notes*), *sk next 3 dc, sc in next ch-3**, V-st in next sc, rep from * across, ending last rep at **, leaving last sc unworked, turn. (*1 dc, 20 [20, 23, 23, 26, 26] sc, 19 [19, 22, 22, 25, 25] V-sts*)

Row 3: Ch 1, shell in first sc, sk next V-st, [shell in next sc, sk next V-st across, sc in last sc, turn. (*1 sc, 19 [19, 22, 22, 25, 25] shells*)

Next rows: [Rep rows 2 and 3 alternately] 2 [2, 4, 4, 6, 6] times. (*1 sc, 17 [17, 18, 18, 19, 19] shells*)

BODICE
X-LARGE, 2X-LARGE, 3X-LARGE, 4X-LARGE SIZES ONLY

Row 1: Ch 3, dc in same sc, *sk next 3 dc, sc in next ch-3**, V-st in next sc, rep from * across, ending last rep at **, dc in last sc, turn. (*3 dc, 17 [17, 18, 18] sc, 16 [16, 17, 17] V-sts*)

Row 2: Ch 3, [shell in next sc, sk next V-st] across, sl st in last dc, turn. (*1 dc, 17 [17, 18, 18] shells*)

Row 3: Ch 3, *sk next 3 dc, sc in next ch-3**, V-st in next sc, rep from * across, ending last rep at **, dc in next sc, dc in last dc, turn. (*3 dc, 17 [17, 18, 18] sc, 16 [16, 17, 17] V-sts*)

Row 4: Ch 3, dc in same dc, sk next dc, [shell in next sc, sk next V-st] across, (sc, dc) in next sc, dc in last dc, turn. (*1 sc, 4 dc, 16 [16, 17, 17] shells*)

Row 5: Ch 1, sc in first dc, sk next dc, *V-st in next sc**, sk next 3 dc, sc in next ch-3, rep from * across, ending last rep at **, sk next dc, sc in last dc, turn. (*18 [18, 19, 19] sc, 17 [17, 18, 18] V-sts*)

Row 6: Ch 1, shell in first sc, sk next V-st, [shell in next sc, sk next V-st] across, sc in last sc, turn. (*1 sc, 17 [17, 18, 18] shells*)

Next rows: [Rep rows 1–6] 1 [1, 0, 0] time(s).

UPPER BODICE
ALL SIZES

Row 1: Ch 3, dc in same sc, *sk next 3 dc, sc in next ch-3**, V-st in next sc, rep from * across, ending last rep at **, dc in last sc, turn. (*3 dc, 17 [17, 18, 18, 19, 19] sc, 16 [16, 17, 17, 18, 18] V-sts*)

Row 2: Ch 3, [shell in next sc, sk next V-st], sl st in last dc, turn. (*1 dc, 17 [17, 18, 18, 19, 19] shells*)

Row 3: Ch 3, *sk next 3 dc, sc in next ch-3**, V-st in next sc, rep from * across, ending last rep at **, dc in next sc, dc in last dc. Fasten off. (*3 dc, 17 [17, 18, 18, 19, 19] sc, 16 [16, 17, 17, 18, 18] V-sts*)

FRONT

Row 1: With WS of Body facing, sk 5 [7, 7, 9, 9, 11] V-sts on last row of Body, join in next sc, ch 1, shell in same sc, sk next V-st, [shell in next sc, sk next V-st] 19 [19, 22, 22, 25, 25] times, sc in next sc, leaving rem sts unworked, turn. (*1 sc, 20 [20, 23, 23, 26, 26] shells*)

Row 2: Ch 3, *sk next 3 dc, sc in next ch-3**, V-st in next sc, rep from * across, ending last rep at **, leaving last sc unworked, turn. (*1 dc, 20 [20, 23, 23, 26, 26] sc, 19 [19, 22, 22, 25, 25] V-sts*)

Row 3: Ch 1, shell in first sc, sk next V-st, [shell in next sc, sk next V-st] across, sc in last sc, turn. (*1 sc, 19 [19, 22, 22, 25, 25] shells*)

Next rows: [Rep rows 2 and 3 alternately] 2 [2, 4, 4, 6, 6] times. (*1 sc, 17 [17, 18, 18, 19, 19] shells at end of last row*)

BODICE

Row 1: Ch 3, dc in same sc, *sk next 3 dc, sc in next ch-3**, V-st in next sc, rep from * across, ending last rep at **, dc in last sc, turn. *(3 dc, 17 [17, 18, 18, 19, 19] sc, 16 [16, 17, 17, 18, 18] V-sts)*

Row 2: Ch 3, [shell in next sc, sk next V-st] across, sl st in last dc, turn. *(1 dc, 17 [17, 18, 18, 19, 19] shells)*

Row 3: Ch 3, *sk next 3 dc, sc in next ch-3**, V-st in next sc, rep from * across, ending last rep at **, dc in next sc, dc in last dc, turn. *(3 dc, 17 [17, 18, 18, 19, 19] sc, 16 [16, 17, 17, 18, 18] V-sts)*

Row 4: Ch 3, dc in same dc, sk next dc, [shell in next sc, sk next V-st] across, (sc, dc) in next sc, dc in last dc, turn. *(1 sc, 4 dc, 16 [16, 17, 17, 18, 18] shells)*

Row 5: Ch 1, sc in first dc, sk next dc, *V-st in next sc**, sk next 3 dc, sc in next ch-3, rep from * across, ending last rep at **, sk next dc, sc in last dc, turn. *(18 [18, 19, 19, 20, 20] sc, 17 [17, 18, 18, 19, 19] V-sts)*

Row 6: Ch 1, shell in first sc, sk next V-st, [shell in next sc, sk next V-st] across, sc in last sc, turn. *(1 sc, 17 [17, 18, 18, 19, 19] shells)*

Row 7: Rep row 1.

RIGHT SHOULDER

Row 1: Ch 3, [shell in next sc, sk next V-st] 6 times, sl st in next sc, leaving rem sts unworked, turn. *(1 dc, 6 shells)*

Row 2: Ch 3, *sk next 3 dc, sc in next ch-3**, V-st in next sc, rep from * across, ending last rep at **, dc in next sc, dc in last dc, turn. *(6 sc, 3 dc, 5 V-sts)*

Row 3: Ch 3, dc in same dc, sk next dc, [shell in next sc, sk next V-st] across, sl st in last sc, turn. *(2 dc, 5 shells)*

Row 4: Ch 3, *sk next 3 dc, sc in next ch-3**, V-st in next sc, rep from * across, sc in last dc, turn. *(1 dc, 6 sc, 5 V-sts)*

Row 5: Ch 1, shell in first sc, sk next V-st, [shell in next sc, sk next V-st] across, sc in last sc, turn. *(1 sc, 5 shells)*

Row 6: Ch 3, dc in same sc, *sk next 3 dc, sc in next ch-3**, V-st in next sc, rep from * across, ending last rep at **, dc in last sc, turn. *(5 sc, 3 dc, 4 V-sts)*

Row 7: Ch 3, [shell in next sc, sk next V-st] across, sc in last dc, turn. *(1 sc, 1 dc, 5 shells)*

Row 8: Ch 3, *sk next 3 dc, sc in next ch-3**, V-st in next sc, rep from * across, ending last rep at **, dc in next sc, dc in last dc, turn. *(5 sc, 3 dc, 4 V-sts)*

Row 9: Ch 3, dc in same dc, sk next dc, [shell in next sc, sk next V-st] across, (sc, dc) in next sc, dc in last dc, turn. *(1 sc, 4 dc, 4 shells)*

Row 10: Ch 1, sc in first dc, sk next dc, *V-st in next sc**, sk next 3 dc, sc in next ch-3, rep from * across, ending last rep at **, sk next dc, sc in last dc, turn. *(6 sc, 5 V-sts)*

Next rows: [Rep rows 5–10 consecutively] twice.

JOINING SHOULDER TO BACK

Working along WS of Right Shoulder and slip stitching along RS of Back, ch 1, *sc in next sc on Shoulder, ch 2, sl st in next sc on Back, 2 dc in same sc on Shoulder, sl st in ch-1 sp of next V-st on Back, dc in same sc of Shoulder**, sk next V-st on Shoulder, rep from * across, ending last rep at **, sl st in next sc of Back. Fasten off. *(1 sc, 6 shells)*

LEFT SHOULDER

Row 1: With WS of Bodice facing, sk next 4 [4, 5, 5, 6, 6] V-sts, join in next sc, ch 3, [shell in next sc, sk next V-st] 6 times, sc in next sc, turn. *(1 sc, 1 dc, 6 shells)*

Row 2: Ch 3, *sk next 3 dc, sc in next ch-3**, V-st in next sc, rep from * across, ending last rep at **, dc in next sc, dc in last dc, turn. *(6 sc, 3 dc, 5 V-sts)*

Row 3: Ch 3, sk next dc, [shell in next sc, sk next V-st] across, (sc, dc) in next sc, dc in last sc, turn. *(1 sc, 3 dc, 5 shells)*

Row 4: Ch 1, sc in first dc, sk next dc, [V-st in next sc, sk next 3 dc, sc in next ch-3] across, sc in last dc, turn. *(6 sc, 5 V-sts)*

Row 5: Ch 1, shell in first sc, sk next V-st, [shell in next sc, sk next V-st] across, sc in last sc, turn. *(1 sc, 5 shells)*

Row 6: Ch 3, dc in same sc, *sk next 3 dc, sc in next ch-3**, V-st in next sc, rep from * across, ending last rep at **, dc in last sc, turn. *(5 sc, 3 dc, 4 V-sts)*

Row 7: Ch 3, [shell in next sc, sk next V-st] across, sk next dc, sc in last dc, turn. *(1 sc, 1 dc, 5 shells)*

Row 8: Ch 3, *sk next 3 dc, sc in next ch-3**, V-st in next sc, rep from * across, ending last rep at **, dc in next sc, dc in last dc, turn. *(5 sc, 3 dc, 4 V-sts)*

Row 9: Ch 3, dc in same dc, sk next dc, [shell in next sc, sk next V-st] across, (sc, dc) in next sc, dc in last dc, turn. *(1 sc, 4 dc, 4 shells)*

Row 10: Ch 1, sc in first dc, sk next dc, *V-st in next sc**, sk next 3 dc, sc in next ch-3, rep from * across, ending last rep at **, sk next dc, sc in last dc, turn. *(6 sc, 6 V-sts)*

Next rows: [Rep rows 5–10 consecutively] twice.

JOINING SHOULDER TO BACK

Working along WS of Left Shoulder and slip stitching along RS of Back, ch 3, sk next 5 [5, 6, 6, 7, 7] V-sts of Back, sl st in next sc of Back, ch 2, sc in first sc of Shoulder, *ch 2, sl st in next ch-1 sp of Back, 2 dc in same sc of Shoulder**, sl st in next sc of Back, dc in same sc of Shoulder, sk next V-st of Shoulder, sc in next sc of Shoulder, rep from * across, ending last rep at **, ch 1, sl st in last dc of Back, ch 1, sl st in last sc of Shoulder. Fasten off. *(1 sc, 6 shells)*

FINISHING
NECKLINE TRIM

With WS of Back neckline facing, join in first sc, (sc, 3 dc) in same sc, *sk next V-st, (sc, 3 dc) in next sc, rep from * across to Shoulder; (sc, 3 dc) evenly sp in ends of rows, sk rows as needed* to Front neckline; rep between * once, join in beg sc. Fasten off.

ARMHOLE TRIM

With WS facing, join in first sc at bottom of armhole, (sc, 3 dc) in same sc, [sk next V-st, (sc, 3 dc) in next sc] across; (sc, 3 dc) evenly sp in ends of rows, sk rows as needed, join in beg sc. Fasten off.

Rep on rem armhole.

BOTTOM TRIM

Working in starting ch on opposite side of row 1, with WS facing at left side, join in ch-3 sp, shell in each ch-3 sp around, join in beg sc. Fasten off. *(50 [54, 60, 64, 70, 74] shells)* ∎

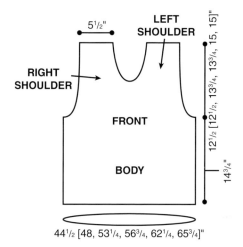

44½ [48, 53¼, 56¾, 62¼, 65¾]"

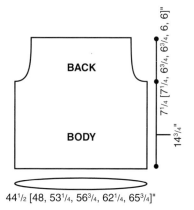

44½ [48, 53¼, 56¾, 62¼, 65¾]"

Soft V-Neck
PULLOVER

SKILL LEVEL

INTERMEDIATE

FINISHED SIZES

Instructions given fit size X-large; changes for
2X-large, 3X-large, 4X-large, 5X-large and
6X-large are in [ ].

FINISHED GARMENT MEASUREMENTS

Bust: 48 inches *(X-large)* [52 inches *(2X-large)*,
56 inches *(3X-large)*, 60 inches *(4X-large)*,
64 inches *(5X-large)*, 68 inches *(6X-large]*

MATERIALS

- Lion Brand Cotton-Ease medium
  (worsted) weight cotton/acrylic
  yarn (3½ oz/207 yds/1000g
  per skein):
    7 [8, 9, 10, 10, 11] skeins #186 maize
- Size I/9/5.5mm crochet hook
  or size needed to obtain gauge
- Tapestry needle
- Stitch markers

GAUGE

16 pattern sts = 4 inches; 9 pattern rows =
4 inches

Take time to check gauge.

PATTERN NOTES

Body of Pullover is crocheted first in rounds.
Front and Back Bodice are then crocheted from
the Body up and joined at shoulders. Sleeves
are crocheted in rounds from bottom to cap,
then sewn in.

Join with slip stitch as indicated unless
otherwise stated.

Chain-1 at beginning of row or round **does not**
count as first stitch unless otherwise stated.

SPECIAL STITCH

Extended single crochet (ext sc): Insert
hook in place indicated, yo, pull up lp, yo,
pull through 1 lp on hook (*first step*), yo, pull
through all lps on hook.

INSTRUCTIONS
PULLOVER
BODY
Rnd 1 (WS): Ch 2, **ext sc** (*see Special Stitch*) in 2nd ch from hook, [ext sc in first step of last ext sc] 190 [206, 222, 238, 254, 270] times, work first step of ext sc, sl st in first step of first ext sc, yo, pull through 2 lps on hook, sl st in first ext sc, turn.

Rnd 2 (RS): Working in **front lps** (*see Stitch Guide*), **ch 1** (*see Pattern Notes*), 2 hdc in first ext sc, sk next ext sc, [2 hdc in front lp of next ext sc, sk next ext sc] around, **join** (*see Pattern Notes*) in top of beg hdc, turn. (*192 [208, 224, 240, 256, 272] hdc*)

Rnd 3: Working in **back lps** (*see Stitch Guide*), ch 1, sc in each hdc around, join in beg sc, turn.

Rnd 4: Ch 1, 2 hdc in first sc, sk next sc, [2 hdc in next sc, sk next sc] around, join in beg hdc, turn.

Next rnds: [Rep rnds 3 and 4 alternately] 18 times.

BACK
Row 1: Ch 1, sl st in each of first 10 [14, 16, 16, 18, 22] hdc, **sc dec** (*see Stitch Guide*) in back lps of next 2 hdc, sc in back lps of each of next 72 [72, 76, 80, 88, 88] hdc, sc dec in back lps of next 2 dc, leaving rem sts unworked, turn. (*74 [74, 78, 82, 90, 90] sc*)

Row 2: Ch 1, hdc in front lp of each of first 2 sc, [sk next sc, 2 hdc in front lp of next sc] across to last 3 sc, sk next sc, hdc in front lp of each of last 2 sc, turn. (*72 [72, 76, 80, 88, 88] hdc*)

Row 3: Ch 1, sk first hdc, sc dec in back lps of next 2 hdc, sc in back lp of each hdc across to last 4 hdc, [sc dec in back lps of next 2 hdc] twice, turn. (*68 [68, 72, 76, 84, 84] sc*)

Row 4: Ch 1, hdc in first sc, [sk next sc, 2 hdc in front lp of next sc] across, hdc in last sc, turn. (*66 [66, 70, 74, 82, 82] hdc*)

Row 5: Ch 1, sk first hdc, sc in back lp of each hdc across to last 2 hdc, sc dec in back lps of last 2 hdc, turn. (*64 [64, 68, 72, 80, 80] sc*)

Row 6: Ch 1, hdc in front lp of each of first 2 sc, [sk next sc, 2 hdc in front lp of next sc] across, turn. (*64 [64, 68, 72, 80, 80] hdc*)

Next rows: [Rep rows 3–6 consecutively] 0 [0, 0, 1, 2, 2] time(s). (*64 [64, 68, 68, 72, 72] hdc at end of last row*)

UPPER BACK
Row 1: Ch 1, sc in back lp of each hdc across, turn.

Row 2: Ch 1, sk first st, 2 hdc in front lp of next sc, [sk next sc, 2 hdc in front lp of next sc] across, turn.

Next rows: [Rep rows 1 and 2] 6 [6, 7, 5, 4, 4] times. At end of last row, fasten off.

FRONT
Row 1: With WS facing, sk 10 [14, 16, 16, 18, 22] hdc from Back on last row of Body, join in next hdc, ch 1, sc dec in back lps of next 2 hdc, sc in back lps of next 72 [72, 76, 80, 88, 88] hdc, sc dec in back lps of next 2 dc, leaving rem sts unworked, turn. (*74 [74, 78, 82, 90, 90] sc*)

Row 2: Ch 1, hdc in front lp of first sc, [sk next sc, 2 hdc in front lp of next sc] across to last 3 sc, sk next sc, sc dec in front lps of last 2 sc, turn. (*72 [72, 76, 80, 88, 88] hdc*)

Row 3: Ch 1, sk first hdc, sc dec in back lps of next 2 hdc, sc in back lp of each hdc across to last 4 hdc, [sc dec in back lps of next 2 hdc] twice, turn. (*68 [68, 72, 76, 84, 84] sc*)

Row 4: Ch 1, hdc in first sc, [sk next sc, 2 hdc in front lp of next sc] across, ending with sc dec in last 2 sc, turn. (*66 [66, 70, 74, 82, 82] hdc*)

Row 5: Ch 1, sk first hdc, sc in back lp of each hdc across to last 2 hdc, sc dec in back lps of last 2 hdc, turn. (*64 [64, 68, 72, 80, 80] sc*)

Next rows: [Rep rows 2–5 consecutively] 0 [0, 0, 1, 2, 2] time(s). (*64 [64, 68, 68, 72, 72] sc at end of last row*)

LEFT FRONT

Row 1: Ch 1, hdc in front lp of each of first 2 sc, [sk next sc, 2 hdc in front lp of next sc] 14 [14, 15, 15, 16, 16] times, sk next sc, hdc in front lp of next sc, leaving rem sc unworked, turn. (*31 [31, 33, 33, 35, 35] sc*)

Row 2: Ch 1, sk first hdc, sc in back lp of each hdc across, turn. (*30 [30, 32, 32, 34, 34] sc*)

Row 3: Ch 1, sk first sc, 2 hdc in front lp of next sc, [sk next sc, 2 hdc in front lp of next sc] across, hdc in last sc, turn. (*29 [29, 31, 31, 33, 33] hdc*)

Rows 4–11: [Rep rows 2–3 alternately] 4 times. (*21 [21, 23, 23, 25, 25] hdc at end of last row*)

Row 12: Rep row 2. (*20 [20, 22, 22, 24, 24] sc*)

Row 13: Ch 1, sk first sc, 2 hdc in front lp of next sc, [sk next sc, 2 hdc in front lp of next sc] across, turn. (*20 [20, 22, 22, 24, 24] hdc*)

Row 14: Ch 1, sc in back lp of each hdc across, turn.

Rows 15–24: [Rep rows 13 and 14 alternately] 5 times.

Row 25: Holding RS of Left Front and Back tog and working through both thicknesses, [sl st in front lp of next sc of Left Front and back lp of corresponding sc of Back at same time] across. Fasten off.

RIGHT FRONT

Row 1: With RS facing, sk next sc on Front, join in next sc, ch 2, [sk next sc, 2 hdc in front lp of next sc] across, turn. (*31 [31, 33, 33, 35, 35] hdc*)

Row 2: Ch 1, sc in back lp of each hdc across, turn. (*30 [30, 32, 32, 34, 34] sc*)

Row 3: Ch 1, sk first sc, hdc in front lp of next sc, [sk next sc, 2 hdc in front lp of next sc] across, turn. (*29 [29, 31, 31, 33, 33] hdc*)

Row 4: Ch 1, sc in back lp of each hdc across to last 2 hdc, sc dec in last 2 hdc, turn. (*28 [28, 30, 30, 32, 32] sc*)

Rows 5–12: [Rep rows 3 and 4 alternately] 4 times. (*20 [20, 22, 22, 24, 24] hdc at end of last row*)

Row 13: Ch 1, sk first sc, 2 hdc in front lp of next sc, [sk next sc, 2 hdc in front lp of next sc] across, turn. (*20 [20, 22, 22, 24, 24] sc*)

Row 14: Ch 1, sc in back lp of each hdc across, turn.

Rows 15–24: [Rep rows 13 and 14 alternately] 5 times. At end of last row, fasten off.

Row 25: Holding RS of Right Front and Back tog and working through both thicknesses, [sl st in front lp of next sc of Right Front and back lp of corresponding sc of Back at same time] across, **do not fasten off**.

NECKLINE TRIM

Working in ends of rows and sts, evenly sp hdc around neck edge, join in beg hdc. Fasten off.

SLEEVE
MAKE 2.

Rnd 1 (WS): Ch 2, ext sc in 2nd ch from hook, [ext sc in first step of last ext sc] 40 [42, 42, 44, 44, 46] times, work first step of ext sc, sl st in first step of first ext sc, yo, pull through 2 lps on hook, sl st in first ext sc, **turn**. (*42 [46, 46, 50, 50, 54] ext sc*)

Rnd 2 (RS): Ch 1, [2 hdc in front lp of next ext sc, sk next ext sc] around, join in top of first hdc, turn. (*42 [46, 46, 50, 50, 54] hdc*)

Rnd 3: Ch 1, 2 sc in joining sl st, sc in back lp of each hdc around, ending with 2 sc in back lp of last hdc, join in beg sc, turn. (*44 [48, 48, 52, 52, 56] sc*)

Rnd 4: Ch 1, hdc in joining sl st, [sk next sc, 2 hdc in front lp of next sc] around, hdc in last sc, join in first hdc, turn. (*44 [48, 48, 52, 52, 56] hdc*)

Rnd 5: Rep rnd 3. (*46 [50, 50, 54, 54, 58] sc*)

Rnd 6: Ch 1, 2 hdc in front lp of first sc, sk next sc, [2 hdc in front lp of next sc, sk next sc] around, join in first hdc, turn. (*46 [50, 50, 54, 54, 58] hdc*)

Rnds 7–38: [Rep rnds 3–6 consecutively] 8 times. *(78 [82, 82, 86, 86, 90] hdc at end of last rnd)*

Rnds 39 & 40: Rep rnds 3 and 4. *(80 [84, 84, 88, 88, 92] hdc at end of last rnd)*

CAP SHAPING

Row 1: Ch 1, sl st in each of first 8 hdc, sc in back lp of each of next 64 [68, 68, 72, 72, 76] hdc, leaving rem hdc unworked, turn. *(64 [68, 68, 72, 72, 76] sc)*

Row 2: Ch 1, sk first sc, hdc in front lp of next sc, [sk next sc, 2 hdc in front lp of next sc] across, hdc in last sc, turn. *(64 [68, 68, 72, 72, 76] hdc)*

Row 3: Ch 1, sk first hdc, sc dec in back lps of next 2 hdc, sc in back lp of each hdc across to last 4 hdc, [sc dec in back lps of next 2 hdc] twice, turn. *(60 [64, 64, 68, 68, 72] sc)*

Row 4: Ch 1, sk first sc, hdc in front lp of next sc, [2 hdc in front lp of next sc, sk next sc] across, turn. *(59 [63, 63, 67, 67, 71] hdc)*

Rows 5 & 6: Rep rows 3 and 4. *(54 [58, 58, 62, 62, 66] hdc at end of last row)*

Row 7: Ch 1, sk first hdc, sc dec in back lps of next 2 hdc, sc in back lp of each hdc across to last 4 hdc, [sc dec in back lps of next 2 hdc] twice, turn. *(50 [54, 54, 58, 58, 62] sc)*

Row 8: Ch 1, hdc in front lp of first sc, [sk next sc, 2 hdc in front lp of next sc] across, hdc in last sc, turn. *(48 [52, 52, 56, 56, 60] hdc)*

Row 9: Ch 1, sk first hdc, [sc dec in back lps of next 2 hdc] twice, sc in back lp of each hdc across to last 6 hdc, [sc dec in back lps of next 2 hdc] 3 times, turn. *(42 [46, 46, 50, 50, 54] hdc)*

Row 10: Ch 1, sk first sc, hdc in front lp of next sc, [sk next sc, 2 hdc in front lp of next sc] across, hdc in last sc, turn. *(40 [44, 44, 48, 48, 52] hdc)*

Next rows: [Rep rows 9 and 10 alternately] 2 [3, 3, 3, 3, 4] times. At end of last row, fasten off. *(24 [20, 20, 24, 24, 20] hdc at end of last row)*

ASSEMBLY

Matching underarm centers and easing to fit, sew Sleeves into armholes. ■

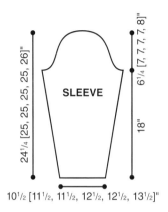

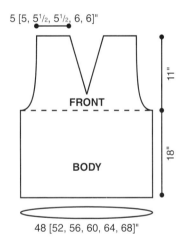

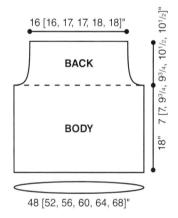

STITCH GUIDE

STITCH ABBREVIATIONS

beg	begin/begins/beginning
bpdc	back post double crochet
bpsc	back post single crochet
bptr	back post treble crochet
CC	contrasting color
ch(s)	chain(s)
ch-	refers to chain or space previously made (i.e., ch-1 space)
ch sp(s)	chain space(s)
cl(s)	cluster(s)
cm	centimeter(s)
dc	double crochet (singular/plural)
dc dec	double crochet 2 or more stitches together, as indicated
dec	decrease/decreases/decreasing
dtr	double treble crochet
ext	extended
fpdc	front post double crochet
fpsc	front post single crochet
fptr	front post treble crochet
g	gram(s)
hdc	half double crochet
hdc dec	half double crochet 2 or more stitches together, as indicated
inc	increase/increases/increasing
lp(s)	loop(s)
MC	main color
mm	millimeter(s)
oz	ounce(s)
pc	popcorn(s)
rem	remain/remains/remaining
rep(s)	repeat(s)
rnd(s)	round(s)
RS	right side
sc	single crochet (singular/plural)
sc dec	single crochet 2 or more stitches together, as indicated
sk	skip/skipped/skipping
sl st(s)	slip stitch(es)
sp(s)	space(s)/spaced
st(s)	stitch(es)
tog	together
tr	treble crochet
trtr	triple treble
WS	wrong side
yd(s)	yard(s)
yo	yarn over

YARN CONVERSION

OUNCES TO GRAMS		GRAMS TO OUNCES	
1	28.4	25	⅞
2	56.7	40	1⅔
3	85.0	50	1¾
4	113.4	100	3½

UNITED STATES		UNITED KINGDOM
sl st (slip stitch)	=	sc (single crochet)
sc (single crochet)	=	dc (double crochet)
hdc (half double crochet)	=	htr (half treble crochet)
dc (double crochet)	=	tr (treble crochet)
tr (treble crochet)	=	dtr (double treble crochet)
dtr (double treble crochet)	=	ttr (triple treble crochet)
skip	=	miss

Single crochet decrease (sc dec): (Insert hook, yo, draw lp through) in each of the sts indicated, yo, draw through all lps on hook.

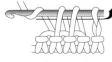

Example of 2-sc dec

Half double crochet decrease (hdc dec): (Yo, insert hook, yo, draw lp through) in each of the sts indicated, yo, draw through all lps on hook.

Example of 2-hdc dec

Reverse Single Crochet (reverse sc): Ch 1. Skip first st. [Working from left to right, insert hook in next st from front to back, draw up lp on hook, yo, and draw through both lps on hook.]

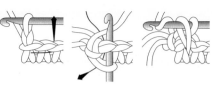

Chain (ch): Yo, pull through lp on hook.

Single crochet (sc): Insert hook in st, yo, pull through st, yo, pull through both lps on hook.

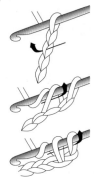

Double crochet (dc): Yo, insert hook in st, yo, pull through st, [yo, pull through 2 lps] twice.

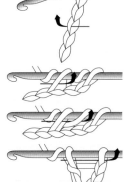

Double crochet decrease (dc dec): (Yo, insert hook, yo, draw loop through, draw through 2 lps on hook) in each of the sts indicated, yo, draw through all lps on hook.

Example of 2-dc dec

Front loop (front lp) Back loop (back lp)

Front Loop   Back Loop

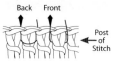

Front post stitch (fp): Back post stitch (bp): When working post st, insert hook from right to left around post st on previous row.

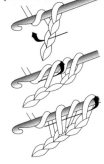

Back   Front

Post of Stitch

Half double crochet (hdc): Yo, insert hook in st, yo, pull through st, yo, pull through all 3 lps on hook.

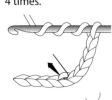

Treble crochet decrease (tr dec): Holding back last lp of each st, tr in each of the sts indicated, yo, pull through all lps on hook.

Example of 2-tr dec

Slip stitch (sl st): Insert hook in st, pull through both lps on hook.

Chain Color Change (ch color change) Yo with new color, draw through last lp on hook.

Double Crochet Color Change (dc color change) Drop first color, yo with new color, draw through last 2 lps of st.

Treble crochet (tr): Yo twice, insert hook in st, yo, pull through st, [yo, pull through 2 lps] 3 times.

Double treble crochet (dtr): Yo 3 times, insert hook in st, yo, pull through st, [yo, pull through 2 lps] 4 times.

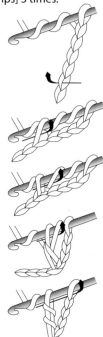

Metric Conversion Charts

METRIC CONVERSIONS

yards	x	.9144	=	metres (m)
yards	x	91.44	=	centimetres (cm)
inches	x	2.54	=	centimetres (cm)
inches	x	25.40	=	millimetres (mm)
inches	x	.0254	=	metres (m)

centimetres	x	.3937	=	inches
metres	x	1.0936	=	yards

INCHES INTO MILLIMETRES & CENTIMETRES (Rounded off slightly)

inches	mm	cm	inches	cm	inches	cm	inches	cm
1/8	3	0.3	5	12.5	21	53.5	38	96.5
1/4	6	0.6	5 1/2	14	22	56	39	99
3/8	10	1	6	15	23	58.5	40	101.5
1/2	13	1.3	7	18	24	61	41	104
5/8	15	1.5	8	20.5	25	63.5	42	106.5
3/4	20	2	9	23	26	66	43	109
7/8	22	2.2	10	25.5	27	68.5	44	112
1	25	2.5	11	28	28	71	45	114.5
1 1/4	32	3.2	12	30.5	29	73.5	46	117
1 1/2	38	3.8	13	33	30	76	47	119.5
1 3/4	45	4.5	14	35.5	31	79	48	122
2	50	5	15	38	32	81.5	49	124.5
2 1/2	65	6.5	16	40.5	33	84	50	127
3	75	7.5	17	43	34	86.5		
3 1/2	90	9	18	46	35	89		
4	100	10	19	48.5	36	91.5		
4 1/2	115	11.5	20	51	37	94		

KNITTING NEEDLES CONVERSION CHART

Canada/U.S.	0	1	2	3	4	5	6	7	8	9	10	10½	11	13	15
Metric (mm)	2	2¼	2¾	3¼	3½	3¾	4	4½	5	5½	6	6½	8	9	10

CROCHET HOOKS CONVERSION CHART

Canada/U.S.	1/B	2/C	3/D	4/E	5/F	6/G	8/H	9/I	10/J	10½/K	N
Metric (mm)	2.25	2.75	3.25	3.5	3.75	4.25	5	5.5	6	6.5	9.0

Plus Size Fashions is published by DRG, 306 East Parr Road, Berne, IN 46711. Printed in USA. Copyright © 2010 DRG.
All rights reserved. This publication may not be reproduced in part or in whole without written permission from the publisher.

RETAIL STORES: If you would like to carry this pattern book or any other DRG publications, visit DRGwholesale.com

Every effort has been made to ensure that the instructions in this publication are complete and accurate.
We cannot, however, take responsibility for human error, typographical mistakes or variations in individual work.
Please visit AnniesCustomerCare.com to check for pattern updates.

ISBN: 978-1-59635-355-8

1 2 3 4 5 6 7 8 9